# THE KING STAG

*Carlo Gozzi*
*translated & adapted by*
*Natalya Baldyga*

**BROADWAY PLAY PUBLISHING INC**
New York
www.broadwayplaypublishing.com
info@broadwayplaypublishing.com

Cover photograph by Ted Simpson

First edition: December 2023
I S B N: 978-0-88145-992-0

Book design: Marie Donovan
Page make-up: Adobe InDesign
Typeface: Palatino

# DEDICATION

For Leo, who particularly liked the bear.

THE KING STAG premiered on 16 February 2017, at Tufts University in Medford, Massachusetts. The cast and creative contributors were:

CIGLIOTTI / BEAR ...................................... Harrison Downs
PARROT / STATUE / DURANDARTE ............. Tony Howard
TARTAGLIA .............................................. Yuval Ben-Hayun
CLARISSA ...................................................... Jacquie Bonnet
PANTALONE . Austyn Williamson (*as* James Williamson)
ANGELA ......................................................... Amanda Rose
BRIGHELLA .................................................... Sean Murphy
SMERALDINA ...................................................... Hanna Carr
TRUFFALDINO................................................Kevin Lombard
LEANDER .................................................... Blair Nodelman
DERAMO ........................................................Paxton Crystal
CHORUS ...........................Stanton Cope, Deborah Greene,
            Connor Hager, Theo Tan, Henry Zumbrunnen

*Director* ...................................................... Natalya Baldyga
*In collaboration with* ............................... Daniel McCusker
*Scenic design* ...................................................... Ted Simpson
*Costume design* ...................................... Linda Ross Girard
*Lighting design* ...................................... Brian Lilienthal
*Sound design* ............................................... Lee Schuna
*Fight choreography* ......................................... Drew Frayre
*Movement choreography* ......................... Danny McCusker
*Improvisation direction* ....................... Matthew McMahan
*Puppet construction* ............................... Jonathan Rooney
*Wig design* ......................................... Rachel Padula Shufelt
*Production Stage Manager* ............................. Mitchel Katz

# ACKNOWLEDGMENTS

This adaptation could not have been possible without the actors and production team at Tufts University who workshopped multiple versions of the text in the winter of 2016 and spring of 2017.

In addition to those mentioned in the production credits, students who contributed their time and various talents were Ana Antolin, James Davis, Celia Gittleman, Anna Robson, Josiah Vasquez, Tara Brooke Watkins, and Irina Yakubovskaya. I am immensely grateful for their willingness to take risks and tackle a wide range of artistic challenges, most of which were new to them. Thanks are also due to my august colleague Laurence Senelick for his encouragement of this and other artistic endeavors.

The play's development also benefited from the keen eye of my assistant director, Peter Secrest, and the shared expertise of colleagues Faye Dupras (puppetry), Joanne Bertelsen Barnett (mime), and Noe Montez (dramaturgy), as well as from the support of my spouse, Ryan Wheeler, who not only provided encouragement, but also solo-parented though the longer-than-usual rehearsal period.

# ADAPTOR'S NOTE

This script is a result of a thirty-year love affair. I first encountered THE KING STAG as a young college student, when I worked in Rome with the Italian director Giovanni Pampiglione. I went on to research and write about Carlo Gozzi in college, graduate school, and beyond. Producing my own translation and adaptation has allowed me to combine my scholarly interests in eighteenth-century theatre with my artistic love of physical theatre.

This play is full of transformations, and through the act of adaptation, it has undergone transformations of its own. I have sought to maintain the wonder of Gozzi's fantastical world, with its magical creatures and enchantments, without presenting a museum piece. This version of THE KING STAG relinquishes the traditional masks of the *commedia dell'arte*, but maintains its improvisation and highly physical performance style. Additionally, by bringing Gozzi's eighteenth-century tale into conversation with the present, I have made some significant changes— women, for example, have a much more active role than in the original. I also drew inspiration from a statement made by playwright Alison Carey, who cautioned theatremakers in 2015 that "Our failure to tell stories of collective activism is literally killing us." This *King Stag* may still revolve around a king, but it is the story of many heroes, each of whom is willing to take a stand against tyranny, even when the situation seems overwhelmingly bleak.

Natalya Baldyga

# HISTORICAL CONTEXT: TRADITION AND TRANSFORMATION IN VENICE

IL RE CERVO (THE KING STAG) may be a delightful comedy full of fairy-tale magic, but it was born from acrimonious conflict and spite. The play, which debuted on January 5, 1762, at the Teatro San Samuele in Venice, represents one salvo in the "Gozzi-Goldoni controversy", an eighteenth-century literary battle between playwrights Carlo Gozzi (1720-1806) and Carlo Goldoni (1707-93). Count Carlo Gozzi had never planned on becoming a playwright; as an impoverished member of the minor aristocracy, Gozzi, one of eleven children, briefly assumed a military career, but primarily spent his time attempting to protect his remaining inheritance from his family's mismanagement. In 1747, he and other conservative young nobles and scholars founded a literary academy meant to oppose "all things modern, especially French"; one of the targets of this semi-serious organization was a new trend in Venetian playwriting, as embodied by erstwhile lawyer and middle-class Francophile Carlo Goldoni (and his rather less talented counterpart, the *abbé* Pietro Chiari). Gozzi and his compatriots objected to new plays that abandoned the literary Tuscan dialect of Dante, Petrarch, and Boccaccio in favor of prose and local dialects; they also disapproved of the move away from improvisation and masks, both essential elements of *commedia*

*dell'arte.* A systematic attack was launched on Chiari
and Goldoni—pamphlets, mock heroical poems, and
satires flew, all of which the Venetian reading public
eagerly consumed. When Goldoni defended himself
by pointing out that his plays were highly successful,
Gozzi promptly produced *L'amore delle tre melarance*
(THE LOVE OF THREE ORANGES, 1761), to prove
to Goldoni that "even the most frivolous material
could find success". Gozzi's first theatrical attempt
not only satirized Goldoni and Chiari personally, but
was, to Gozzi's immense gratification, also a huge hit.
With this, the first of his ten *fiabe* (fairy tales), Gozzi
had become a playwright and the self-proclaimed
"defender of *commedia dell'arte*".

As is usually the case with theatrical controversies,
more was at stake than aesthetics. With his plays,
Gozzi was resisting not only cultural changes, but
also significant political and economic shifts that
were occurring in Venetian society. Transformation
is at the heart of THE KING STAG, as it is in many of
his *fiabe*, and it is represented by Gozzi as something
to be feared and resisted. In the eighteenth century
the status of the Venetian aristocracy was changing;
impoverished nobles were forced to sell seats on the
Grand Council to wealthy families of common descent,
while new members of the ruling class renounced their
tradesman origins. Gozzi's *fiabe* reflect the resistance
of the Venetian aristocracy to changing times. Socially,
the divide between characters is clearly demarcated.
In the original version of THE KING STAG, Deramo,
the king, is almost painfully noble, and the majority
of the play's broad physical comedy falls to the
lower classes, represented by stock figures of the
*commedia dell'arte*, who are their silliest when they are
attempting to imitate the manners of their betters.
Conversely, when Carlo Goldoni began, in the 1740s,

to write scripted plays in the Venetian dialect and to alter traditional *commedia* characters (toning down their more disreputable qualities), he introduced new social types to the stage, creating respectable middle-class characters to which a significant portion of his audience members might relate. Goldoni's plays therefore presented a challenge to the social order— and to Count Gozzi—by presenting middle-class characters who are the moral center of the play and aristocratic characters who do not necessarily behave well or according to their station. Gozzi accused Goldoni of debasing the aristocracy in order to pander to the lowest common denominator in the audience, and his *fiabe* provided him with a means of righting this perceived wrong.

Gozzi also objected to Goldoni's use of French theatrical models, as he was particularly sensitive about the encroachment of French into the Italian literary landscape and the trendy employment of French words and phrases. French also carried less-than-savory associations (for conservative aristocrats) with the *philosophes*, the "irreligious" and dangerously democratic philosophers of the French Enlightenment. Indeed, that which appears to alarm Gozzi most of all is the potential societal transformations that might be affected by the incursion of Enlightenment ideas into the Venetian Republic, which, despite its rhetorical self-positioning as a bastion of political liberty, was in fact controlled by a conservative oligarchy resistant to social change. In his *fiabe*, Gozzi dismisses Enlightenment beliefs that the betterment of mankind will happen at the hands of science and philosophy and mocks those who would flaunt tradition in the name of progress. For Gozzi, adaptation—whether artistic, socio-political, cultural, or ideological— remained a troubling prospect. It is no wonder that transformations in THE KING STAG are fraught with danger.

Our adaptation of THE KING STAG, unlike Gozzi's original, embraces change, viewing transformation as an act that is sometimes dangerous and sometimes beneficial. And in fact, Gozzi's plays hardly preserved the *commedia* in any sort of "pure" form. With his *fiabe*, Gozzi exploited the well-established fascination for folktales in eighteenth-century Venice, as well as the fashionable orientalist craze sparked by *The Thousand and One Nights* (1704-17). Additionally, the alterations that Gozzi makes to *commedia* characters move his creations away from the traditional form that he purports to defend—like Goldoni, Gozzi softens stock characters, stripping out the lewdness and vulgarity that was a feature of traditional *commedia*. Gozzi's combination of nostalgia (for the traditional aspects of *commedia*) and novelty (through "exotic" settings) created an entirely new genre, despite his use of conventional *commedia* characters, one that would later inspire the Romantics of the nineteenth century. Change will come, whether we like it or no, and, despite the failures of the eighteenth century, it is worth remembering that which it sought to usher in—a celebration of reason and the pursuit of knowledge, a critique of authoritarianism, and an insistence on the equal value of all human beings.

# PRODUCTION NOTES

This adaptation of THE KING STAG had its world premiere at Tufts University, in March 2017; it was directed by Natalya Baldyga, in collaboration with choreographer Daniel McCusker. Some stage directions reflect the original staging in the Tufts University Balch Arena Theater, a small arena stage with an upper concourse and five voms. Adapt as needed.

The play is meant to be seamless, with no blackouts. Scene changes should be out in the open and integrated into the world of the play.

The original production did not use masks, which made magical transformations more challenging. Figuring them out, however, was part of the fun. We created transformation dreamscapes, with slow-motion choreography that allowed the audience to witness the transformations as they happened. Once transformations were complete, we snapped back into real time. I've noted what we did, but you are welcome to come up with your own solutions for theatrical magic. Whatever you choose to do, don't try to hide the transformations—lean into them and make them exciting to watch.

Following Gozzi, there's no fourth wall. Actors should acknowledge the audience, even when they're in a scene with another person. Enjoy the asides, let the audience know how you feel, try to get them on your side.

Rather than writing out those scenes that Gozzi indicates should be improvised, I've maintained these as places for improvisation. Improvised moments are indicated by italics.

Gozzi calls for two stags, a bear, a parrot, and a laughing statue. We added a kinesthetic, sentient forest. Our stags had headdresses that left the actors' faces exposed, our bear was a rather tall (6'10) actor in a full blue bear suit, and our statue was an actor whose exposed skin was covered in bronze body paint. We had a wonderfully articulate (and highly realistic) parrot puppet, but if puppets won't work for you, that's fine. Again, lean into the theatricality of the world and enjoy discovering how you'd like to make Gozzi's creatures come to life.

# CHARACTERS & SETTING

CIGLIOTTI, *storyteller, serves as Prologue (also plays* BEAR)

DURANDARTE, *a magician (also plays laughing* STATUE *and controls* PARROT *puppet)*

DERAMO, *king of Serendipity, in love with* ANGELA *(also plays* OLD MAN)

ANGELA, *an intellectual, daughter of* PANTALONE, *in love with* DERAMO

PANTALONE, *second minister of* DERAMO

TARTAGLIA, *first minister, in love with* ANGELA

CLARISSA, *a romantic, daughter of* TARTAGLIA, *in love with* LEANDER

LEANDER, *a knight, daughter of* PANTALONE, *in love with* CLARISSA

BRIGHELLA, *the king's butler*

SMERALDINA, BRIGHELLA'*s sister, sometimes in love with* TRUFFALDINO

TRUFFALDINO, *a bird catcher, in love with* SMERALDINA

CHORUS, *creates the world of the play through movement* (CHORUS *members play* DEER, GUARDS, *and* SENTIENT TREES)[1]

---

1    SENTIENT TREES *can be eliminated, if necessary, but they add considerably to the fun and magic of the play. The actors playing* CLARISSA *and* SMERALDINA *can also double as* TREES.

*Place: The Kingdom of Serendipity and its nearby countryside.*

*Time: Not the eighteenth century.*

*Roles are open in terms of age, physical ability, race, and ethnicity. Some characters are gendered; gender can be flexible, but a character's gender should not be changed for the sole purpose of making a relationship heteronormative.*

# ACT ONE

## Scene 1

*(Setting: An open space, serving as various rooms in the palace of* DERAMO, *King of Serendipity.)*

*(At rise:* CIGLIOTTI *enters the house, greets the audience— cuts through the aisles, stepping over audience members' feet, shaking hands, high fives, etc.).*

CIGLIOTTI: *(Improvising)* Hello! Hi! Excuse me, sorry... Oh, good evening, madam— Nice to see you, sir— Nice jacket! —Say, come here often? *(And so forth)*

*(*PARROT *enters through the house, taking a different path from* CIGLIOTTI. *Investigates audience, squawks occasional comments to audience members.)*

*(*CIGLIOTTI *and the* PARROT *make it to the center of the stage.* CIGLIOTTI *looks around beaming. Continues to greet audience members. Attempts to get the* PARROT, *who is flapping around the space, to settle down.)*

PARROT: Start the show, Cigolotti!

*(*CIGLIOTTI *remembers that he is supposed to be providing the prologue. He hushes the* PARROT. *It subsides.)*

CIGLIOTTI: *(Clears throat, adopts grand tone)* Dear friends, I have come here today to tell you of wonderful things! Five years ago—to the day—a famous magician arrived in this very city, here in the kingdom of Serendipity, where you are so kind as to be joining

us. The magician practiced black magic! He practiced
white magic! He practiced red, green, purple, blue,
yellow, and even turquoise magic! His name *(Dramatic
pause)* was Durandarte—and I am his faithful servant.
*(Bows theatrically)* As soon as Deramo, our king, heard
of my master's arrival, he invited him to his court and
treated him with great kindness, showering him with
gifts, and banquets, and festivals, and gold, and—
*(Drops his grand tone)* Look, I don't have time to list
everything the king did for my master, so I'll just tell
you about the magic secrets. *(Resumes "important" tone)*
The powerful magician gave the king an astonishing
gift—two secrets handed down from the Queen of the
Fairies—two remarkable, spectacular, amazing secrets
that defy description *(Gets off track and loses grand tone
again)* really, just astonishing, astonishing secrets, you
won't *believe* it when I tell you what they are...

*(PARROT squawks and makes some sort of threatening
movement.)*

CIGLIOTTI: Except that I'm not supposed to tell you,
because then they won't be a surprise when you see
them. Durandarte—the magician—was very clear
about this. "Cigolotti" —that's me— "Cigolotti," he
said, "woe be to you if you reveal to anyone the two
prodigious secrets that I have given to the King of
Serendipity earlier than the year 2017![2] Make your
living as a storyteller and tend to me while I spend the
next five years as a parrot. *(Aside)* Listen, if you don't
want to spend time as a parrot, don't reveal magic
secrets that were given to you by the Queen of the
Fairies. Amiright?

*(PARROT menaces CIGLIOTTI. He gets back on track.)*

CIGLIOTTI: When my sentence is done, carry me—in

the form of a parrot—into the Forest of Noname,[3] so that I may help to punish a most treacherous deed! Remember," said Durandarte, "in the year [2017], on the day of [February 16], you must release me, so that I may come to the aid of a brave and clever woman in her hour of need. Do this and you shall gain your heart's desire!" After this pronouncement, he abandoned his human form, and much to my amazement became a beautiful parrot. *(Stage whisper)* The Parrot is a magician! Magician—parrot, parrot— Magician.

*(PARROT preens; squawks.* CIGLIOTTI *resumes grand tone)*

CIGLIOTTI: Pay attention, therefore, my friends, to the astonishing events to follow! I will now release Durandarte, the parrot magician, into the Forest of Noname, with the hopes that it will bring everyone (including myself) their hearts' desires!

*(CIGLIOTTI makes a sweeping gesture; the PARROT circles the space and flies off.)*

*(CIGLIOTTI surveys the space and snaps his fingers. Five GUARDS march in and take their places over the entrances to the voms—we are now in a hall of the palace.)*

*(CIGLIOTTI performs another sweeping gesture, summoning the other characters onstage. The other characters interact as they cross the stage—ANGELA and DERAMO are conversing—CLARISSA and LEANDER are canoodling— SMERALDINA and TRUFFALDINO are having a ridiculous flirtation/argument—PANTALONE trundles through greeting everyone, dictating notes to BRIGHELLA, who attempts to keep up.)*

---

3        *Fake Italian. Pronounced "Noh-nah-meh." Gozzi's original is the Forest of Roncislappe. Feel free to make up your own forest name, if you'd like.*

*(Everyone except* CLARISSA *exits; she stares dreamily off in the direction that* LEANDER *exited.* CIGLIOTTI *makes a gesture to signal "dramatic entrance sound cue," then exits.)*

*(Big dramatic sound cue as* TARTAGLIA *enters and strikes a dramatic pose appropriate for a scheming, scenery-chewing villain. Sound cue startles* CLARISSA, *who gives audience a "was that really necessary?" look.)*

TARTAGLIA:[4] *(Approaching* CLARISSA*)* Well, well, well, my girl, we've been lucky indeed in the kingdom of Serendipity. You are a lady-in-waiting, and I, Tartaglia, am prime minister—feared by all and loved by King Deramo. Today is the day to rise even higher, and, if you obey me, you will be crowned queen this very day.

CLARISSA: Queen? What? How?

TARTAGLIA: Yes, yes, yes, queen, queen, queen! You know that King Deramo, four years ago, after having interviewed two thousand, seven hundred, and forty-eight princesses in his secret chamber rejected them all, for who knows what reason, and decided he would never marry.

CLARISSA: I still don't see how I could be queen. It's inconceivable that he would want to marry me after rejecting two thousand, seven hundred, and forty-eight princesses.

TARTAGLIA: Nitwit! I know what I'm talking about—let me finish! Yesterday I finally persuaded him to marry, by stressing to him that he has no child, no heir to the throne, and that the people are discontented and mutinous. *(Aside)* I might have made that last part up.

CLARISSA: I don't think the people are discontented and—

---

4        *In traditional commedia,* TARTAGLIA *is a stutterer; I've chosen to give* TARTAGLIA *a verbal tic (repetition of words), as a nod to the original, while seeking to avoid the troublesome trope of indicating an evil nature by giving the character a disability.*

TARTAGLIA: But he insists on questioning any candidates for queen in his secret chamber first.

CLARISSA: But haven't we run out of princesses at this point?

TARTAGLIA: Yes, yes, yes, because there are no more princesses to be found, he has decided to question *all* the available young women in the kingdom, and he'll choose whomever he likes.

CLARISSA: *(Aside)* I don't like where this going.

TARTAGLIA: The names of two hundred young women were placed in an urn, your name emerged first, and now you must ready yourself for his interrogation.

CLARISSA: *(Aside)* Interrogation??

TARTAGLIA: The king regards me highly, you're my daughter, you're not hideous; if you do at all well, I am certain that today you will become queen, and I, your father, will be the most resplendent man in the world!

*(TARTAGLIA practices being the most resplendent man in the world; nodding graciously from side to side, waving regally, etc.)*

CLARISSA: Oh, Father, no! Please, release me from this ordeal, I beg you.

TARTAGLIA: What! What! What! Now, listen you little minx, present yourself to the king immediately, and do well in the interview—

CLARISSA: *(Aside)* Now it's an interview?

TARTAGLIA: —otherwise you'll be sorry! Why this hesitation? Is there something you're hiding? Hmmm? Hmmm? Hmmm? Is there something you're not telling me?

CLARISSA: No, nothing…but I have a premonition! I won't do well in the interview…interrogation… questioning. I can't do it. I'll be rejected.

TARTAGLIA: What, what, what premonition? What
rejection? Impossible. The king regards me too highly.
Come, come, come, let's go, it's time. He awaits you in
the secret chamber.

(TARTAGLIA *grabs* CLARISSA's *arm.)*

CLARISSA: *(Pulls free)* I can't, Father, I can't!

TARTAGLIA: Do as I say or I will lock you up and throw
away the key!

(TARTAGLIA *grabs for* CLARISSA *again, but she evades him.)*

CLARISSA: Father, please, I couldn't possibly do well!
*(In desperation)* I'll tell you truth...I'm in love with
Leander. Utterly, completely, desperately in love. I
can't possibly hide my love from the king.

TARTAGLIA: *(Furious, recoiling)* With Leander, the
daughter of Pantalone, the second minister? Leander,
a simple knight? Leander?? You would prefer the
spawn of Pantalone over a monarch! Are you my
daughter? Despicable, unworthy daughter of the
mighty Tartaglia! Listen to me—if you reveal this vile
love in front of the king—if you don't make him choose
you—I'll, I'll, I'll—

(TARTAGLIA *lunges for* CLARISSA; *she holds up her hand,
stopping him.)*

CLARISSA: Wait, Father, there's something else. If I do
what you say, I'll also be betraying Angela, my dearest
friend in the whole world. She's hopelessly in love
with the king! Please, please don't make me do this!

TARTAGLIA: *(Another dramatic recoil)* Angela,
Pantalone's older daughter, loves the king? *(Aside)*
Angela! Oh my heart! I was planning to make her
my bride! *(Advances on* CLARISSA) Clarissa, listen, and
tremble. If you do not immediately present yourself
to the king—without mentioning a single word about
your so-called love for Leander—and if he does not

choose you as his wife—you shall fall a victim to my fury!

CLARISSA: I will obey you. You will be repaid by seeing me rejected and shamed.

TARTAGLIA: *(Seizing her and hustling her offstage)* No more stalling! Don't make me lock you up! Nitwit! Tittle-tattle! Flibbertigibbet! Minx!

CLARISSA: *(To the audience)* What will I do? Heaven help me!

*(CLARISSA and TARTAGLIA exit out one vom, as PANTALONE and ANGELA enter from another.)*

PANTALONE: It's a complete mystery, my dear daughter, a complete mystery! No one knows what's going on. Two thousand, seven hundred, and forty-eight princesses have been rejected by our king. He leads them into his secret chamber, asks them three or four questions, and then politely sends them on their way. Up until now—and I've worked for him a long time—I've always found him to be a wise and kind and intelligent prince. I don't know what's gotten into him!

ANGELA: Father, why must I take part in this shameful exercise?

*(At various points during the following, ANGELA will attempt to break in, but there is no stopping PANTALONE as he paces and frets.)*

PANTALONE: Oh, dear heart, I threw myself to my knees, I begged him, I pleaded with him to give you a special dispensation from having to appear before him. I told him, and it's most assuredly true, that we are of decent enough stock, that we are honest people, but that we are not worthy of competing for such an honor. No response! And then do you know what he said? That it would not be fair, because it was his will that every woman should be seen, and my daughter should not be given the privilege of avoiding the trial that everyone else has to face. I begged, and begged again, I tried everything. He stood firm, had your name placed in the urn along with all the others, and it was drawn third. What can I do? You must go. Do you think that I want to expose you to court gossip? To have people whispering and speculating as to what made you unworthy and why you were rejected? It breaks my heart, Angela, it breaks my heart.

ANGELA: Oh, Father. I am less concerned with whether I am worthy or unworthy of such a high honor. I wonder instead why I must present myself in such a way to prove that I am worthy. What is he looking for? Sincerity? Faithfulness? If he is looking for these— and love—doesn't he realize that there's already someone—

PANTALONE: Now, now, we may not know his purposes, but he's always been just in the past. There must be some reason for this competition.

ANGELA: I don't care what his reasons are, he shouldn't ask me to do this.

(PANTALONE *stops fretting, and focuses on* ANGELA.)

PANTALONE: Angela, my girl, is there something you want to tell me?

ANGELA: No. Yes. Perhaps.

PANTALONE: Come, come, my child, unburden yourself.

ANGELA: Oh, Father, my beloved Father.

PANTALONE: Go on, my child. Trust the father who loves you more than life itself.

ANGELA: So be it. I will confess the truth to you. (*A breath*) Dearest father, I have been so bold as to fall helplessly in love with my king. To be rejected by him

would break my heart—not because I wish to marry
a king, I have no such ambition—but because I could
not bear to be despised by the person who is my very
heart, my life.

PANTALONE: Oh, my poor dear girl.

ANGELA: *(Looks at her father affectionately, makes a gesture
to console him—pats his hand or kisses the top of his head)*
Never mind. It's only a short ordeal. It will all be over
soon. What concerns me more is Clarissa. Her father
hopes to exploit this peculiar competition—and his
own daughter—to get closer to the throne. Also—

PANTALONE: What is it, my child?

ANGELA: He, Tartaglia, is constantly watching me and
sighing. And, this morning, he tried to persuade me
that I should pretend to be sick, so that I wouldn't have
to present myself to the king.

PANTALONE: Well, that's a fine kettle of fish! I hardly
know what to say.

ANGELA: I'm certain I'm not imagining it.

PANTALONE: Oh, no—I trust your judgment, daughter.
Oh, dear, oh dear. We will speak of this later, believe
you me! *(Places an arm around her)* But now I'm afraid
we must go, because it's almost time for you to see the
king.

ANGELA: Love, give me strength!

*(ANGELA and PANTALONE exit.)*

*(SMERALDINA and BRIGHELLA enter. Both are dressed in
an outlandish fashion. SMERALDINA has a huge fan; she has
decorated her outfit with enormous flowers and plumes of
feathers—she is a caricature of fashionable lady.)*

BRIGHELLA: Come on, hold your head a bit higher!
Don't hold your arms so awkwardly! What are you
doing with your feet? I've been trying to teach you for

an hour and you're worse than ever! You're flopping around like a fish!

SMERALDINA: Oh, you're so silly! Just wait till the court sees me—simply *everyone* will fall in love with me, and all the fashionable ladies will want to dress just like me, and then you will have to teach *them* how to act like *me*.

(SMERALDINA *practices walking, waving, curtsying, fainting, simpering—with various interventions by* BRIGHELLA. SMERALDINA *is delighted by her own performance.*)

BRIGHELLA: Would you please be serious?! This occasion shouldn't be taken lightly!

SMERALDINA: Oh, relax!

BRIGHELLA: Relax? If the king falls in love with you, you will become queen *this very day*, and I, your brother, will no longer be a butler but practically commander-in-chief!

SMERALDINA: Oh, just you wait. I'll make him fall in love with me. For three days now I've been practicing the most romantic ballads. And I do best sighs and the best fainting in the world! (*She begins a spectacular combination of singing and sighing and fainting.*)

BRIGHELLA: Stop! Stop! Please stop! Just...stop.

(SMERALDINA *loses her balance and collapses in a heap.* BRIGHELLA *heaves her to her feet.*)

BRIGHELLA: I hope to heaven that everything turns out the way we planned; but

(*Looks at* SMERALDINA, *who is has resumed practicing curtsying and waving, etc.*)

BRIGHELLA: Lord above… That's enough! Into the breach!

SMERALDINA: Ready or not, Kingy, here I come!

(BRIGHELLA *and* SMERALDINA *start to exit, but are stopped when* TRUFFALDINO *enters, dressed as a birdcatcher; a ridiculous number of bird whistles are hung around his neck.)*[5]

(TRUFFALDINO *encounters* SMERALDINA *and* BRIGHELLA, *laughs loudly upon seeing* SMERALDINA'*s comic attire; asks where she's going.*)

(BRIGHELLA *says that* SMERALDINA'*s going to present herself in the king's chambers as part of the competition to be the king's bride.*)

(SMERALDINA *explains that she will soon be queen!*)

(TRUFFALDINO *laughs even harder, he mocks* SMERALDINA—*how on earth could she attract a king?*)

(SMERALDINA: *easily! She demonstrates her astonishing abilities—comic business ensues.*)

(BRIGHELLA: *effusive praise as he critically dissects her performance.*)

(TRUFFALDINO *mocks her with his own take on the performance—doesn't understand why she prefers the king to him.*)

(SMERALDINA *gives an example of something fabulous that the king owns.*)

(TRUFFALDINO *counters with something [absurd] that he has brought her in the past.*)

(SMERALDINA *remembers it wistfully.*)

(BRIGHELLA *reminds her what was wrong with* TRUFFALDINO'*s gift.*)

5       *The dialogue in this section is improvised, as in Gozzi's original.* SMERALDINA *and* TRUFFALDINO *should take audience suggestions for* SMERALDINA'*s talent, the king's treasure, and* TRUFFALDINO'*s gifts to* SMERALDINA. *(If you have children in the audience, I highly recommend asking them.) The position at court that* SMERALDINA *offers to* TRUFFALDINO *at the end of the scene should also change nightly.*

(SMERALDINA *also remembers the gift's flaws.*)

(BRIGHELLA *reminds her that she doesn't have to lower herself to the level of this wretched creature; offers his arm to* SMERALDINA*; they grandly make as if to leave.*)

(TRUFFALDINO *protests that she had promised to marry him—how could she do this to him?*)

(SMERALDINA *softens, comforts him tragically; promises to give him an important position once she has become queen.*)

(SMERALDINA *and* BRIGHELLA *exit grandly.* TRUFFALDINO *is left in despair, in a little heap on one side of the stage.* LEANDER *and* CLARISSA *enter.*)

LEANDER: Clarissa, Clarissa, please stop!

CLARISSA: Oh, Leander, what a disaster!

LEANDER: Please, Clarissa, don't cry.

CLARISSA: There's an awful lot to cry about. My father knows that I love you and he's still insisting that I present myself to the king for his horrible wife competition.

LEANDER: I'm sure we'll be all right. He's already rejected two thousand, seven hundred, and forty-eight princesses. I can't imagine that he'll choose you.

CLARISSA: I'm sorry, what was that?

LEANDER: I just mean, that if he's already rejected two thousand, seven hundred, and forty-eight princesses, he must have pretty refined taste.

CLARISSA: I see.

LEANDER: (*Oblivious to the danger*) I mean, really, think about it, he's rejected two *thousand*, seven hundred, and forty-eight *princesses*. And you're not even a princess—you're only the daughter of his prime minister.

CLARISSA: *(Icily)* Well, then, if I'm so repulsive, then there's nothing to worry about, is there?

LEANDER: Wait, what?

CLARISSA: I mean, how could I even think there was any danger of the king choosing such a hideous, unsightly, stomach-turning hobgoblin.

LEANDER: Clarissa, I didn't mean—

CLARISSA: No, that's fine. I understand. How could I even think to aspire to a king…let alone the daughter of the king's *second* minister.

LEANDER: That's not what I was saying. And my father is a very important man.

CLARISSA: Second. Minister.

LEANDER: Well, at least he would never marry his daughter to someone she didn't love. *(Looks at her)* Especially if she loved someone else. And was the most amazing, kind, passionate, beautiful, graceful, exquisite woman in the whole entire world.

CLARISSA: Oh, Leander.

LEANDER: Oh, Clarissa.

*(CLARISSA and LEANDER cling to each other.)*

LEANDER: What are we going to do? Of course the king is going to pick you. How could he not? You're the most wonderful woman in Serendipity.

CLARISSA: Oh, Leander!

LEANDER: Oh, Clarissa!

CLARISSA: I'll go to my father one last time. He can't do this to us. He can't.

*(CLARISSA kisses LEANDER, then runs off, starts to exit, but stops. They look at each other desperately. CLARISSA leaves. LEANDER, completely dejected, slumps to the floor.)*[6]

6       *This section is improvised, as in Gozzi's original.*

(LEANDER, *on one side of the stage, sadly proclaims her fears that* CLARISSA, *her love, will be chosen by the king because of her great beauty, and that she will remain disappointed in love.*)

(TRUFFALDINO, *on the other side of the stage, profoundly afflicted, gives a highly detailed description of the beauties of* SMERALDINA—*his depiction of her is rather unappealing; he fears that the choice of the king will fall on her; he despairs.*)

(LEANDER *worries whether* CLARISSA *will show a lack of constancy; decides however that the ambition of* TARTAGLIA *has forced* CLARISSA *to present herself in the chamber of the king.*)

(TRUFFALDINO, *on the other side of the stage, berates* SMERALDINA *for her inconstancy; he decides that she has been forced by* BRIGHELLA, *her brother, to appear before the king.*)

(*Both of them weep. They become aware of each other—rush to each other and embrace in sympathy; much weeping.*)

(LEANDER *insists that* CLARISSA *will be chosen by the king.*)

(TRUFFALDINO *maintains that the choice will be* SMERALDINA.)

(LEANDER *and* TRUFFALDINO *become more heated about their opinions—a debate ensues about the relative merits of* CLARISSA *and* SMERALDINA.)

(LEANDER *insists that* CLARISSA *will be chosen because of her astonishing talents and abilities; she lists something particularly impressive.*)

(TRUFFALDINO: *counters with a bizarre ability of* SMERALDINA's.)

(*An impasse.* LEANDER *and* TRUFFALDINO *stomp back to their sides of the stage.*)

---

LEANDER *can take audience suggestions for* CLARISSA's *talents.*

(LEANDER *hopes, reflecting on the two thousand, seven hundred, and forty-eight women presented to the king in vain, that* CLARISSA *won't be the exception. He exits.*)

(TRUFFALDINO: *if the king rejects* SMERALDINA, *he won't be able to tolerate receiving a certain refusal.*)

(CIGLIOTTI *enters and snaps his fingers at* TRUFFALDINO— *he gestures for* TRUFFALDINO *to join him offstage.*)

(*As they exit,* BRIGHELLA *rolls on a large pouffe, checks its placement, exits.*)

(CIGLIOTTI *and* TRUFFALDINO *bring on a pedestal.* BRIGHELLA *reenters and is annoyed that* TRUFFALDINO *is encroaching on his turf;* CIGLIOTTI *tells him he's making a fuss over nothing as they exit.* TRUFFALDINO *stands on the pouffe and makes rude gestures in the direction they exited.*)

(TRUFFALDINO *runs off as* BRIGHELLA *and* CIGLIOTTI *reenter carrying the* STATUE, *which they place on the pedestal.* BRIGHELLA *fusses over the* STATUE, *checking its placement and dusting it vigorously.* CIGLIOTTI *shoos him offstage.*)

(CIGLIOTTI *then makes a sweeping gesture. Light change as the* GUARDS *march on—each* GUARD *marches to their individual platform over a vom, and, in unison, the* GUARDS *release rich tapestries which roll down, masking the entrances to the voms.*)

(*We are now in the royal chambers of* DERAMO, *the king.* CIGLIOTTI *checks to make sure all is in its place, exits, cuing the* GUARDS *as he leaves.*)

(*End of scene*)

## Scene 2

*(Setting: Along with the tapestries masking the entrances to the voms [with the* GUARDS *standing over them on platforms],* DERAMO's *secret chamber contains the set pieces brought on at the end of the previous scene—a large, round nineteenth-century style pouffe [large enough for two people to sit on] and a pedestal [upon which stands the* STATUE*].)*

*(The* GUARDS *signal the entrance of* DERAMO *with impressive, military-sounding business.* DERAMO *enters.)*

DERAMO: *(To the audience)* Here I am, on the advice of my minister Tartaglia, in a difficult situation—I must choose a wife—in the most preposterous of ways. *(Turning to the* STATUE*)* All I can do is place myself in your hands, worthy gift of the magician Durandarte. You have defended me through your laughter, which has revealed the falsehoods and bad faith of those who sought to take advantage of me. Do not abandon me now. Continue to give me your sign, let your laughter reveal the truth. *(To the audience)* I would prefer to leave no successor to my throne, than to be joined in marriage to someone who cares only about my rank and position. After such a long search, it seems impossible that I will ever find someone who truly cares for me. *(Gathers himself)* But duty calls. Let us see what the daughter of Tartaglia feels.

*(The* GUARDS *repeat their entrance business.* CLARISSA *enters and curtsies.)*

DERAMO: Clarissa, please sit. Do not let the presence of your king intimidate you. You may speak openly here. Please—sit.

CLARISSA: Your majesty, I thank you for your great goodness, and only because I must obey you, I will sit in your presence. *(She sits.)*

DERAMO: The merits of your father, both in war and peace, are great, and you should consider yourself a worthy candidate for a noble marriage. Your father insists that I must choose a wife today, for the good of the kingdom, and I have agreed to do so. But first I would like to know from you, if you would truthfully care for such a marriage?

CLARISSA: Who would not be pleased by such an illustrious match, to such a generous king, a model of virtue, and a paragon of goodness?

*(CLARISSA is pleased to have come up with this non-answer answer. DERAMO, unseen by CLARISSA, checks the STATUE; it shows no sign of movement.)*

DERAMO: No, Clarissa. Your remarks are too general.

CLARISSA: What do you mean, my lord?

DERAMO: I want to know your thoughts. I am sure that many women would be grateful to marry their king, and yet, perhaps Clarissa does not share that feeling.

CLARISSA: Oh, your majesty...

DERAMO: Clarissa, I ask you again. Would you welcome such a marriage?

CLARISSA: *(Aside)* Oh, Heavens! He's so insistent! *(To DERAMO)* And why, my lord, should you believe that I would be so foolish as to be displeased by achieving the great fortune desired by so many women?

*(DERAMO, checking the STATUE, which remains still:)*

DERAMO: Your speech, Clarissa, is still too ambiguous. I wish to know your feelings. Would you welcome a marriage with me or not?

CLARISSA: *(Aside)* Why must my father make me a liar! *(To DERAMO)* Yes, I would welcome it, beloved king.

*(STATUE's face contorts briefly with laughter; it then recomposes itself. DERAMO notes its reaction.)*

DERAMO: *(Gently)* Clarissa, are you afraid to say: "I would not welcome it," because you do not wish to disrespect your king?

*(DERAMO sees something in CLARISSA's face.)*

DERAMO: Or—is there something else? Does your heart perhaps yearn for another?

CLARISSA: *(Not able to look at him. Each sentence gets harder to say.)* No, my king, I love only you. I know that I am not worthy to stand at the side of a king, but, if I were, I would long for you alone, and I have never loved another.

*(STATUE silently laughs more broadly; then recomposes itself. DERAMO sees it react.)*

DERAMO: Very well, you may go, Clarissa. I understand. Let me interview the others before I announce my decision.

CLARISSA: *(Rises, curtsies)* Thank you, my lord. *(Aside)* Oh, please don't let him choose me! All I want is Leander!

*(The GUARDS perform impressive military-sounding exit business. CLARISSA exits.)*

DERAMO: I thought for a moment that I had found someone sincere. Poor thing. *(Turns to the STATUE)* Oh, wondrous marvel, thank you for revealing her secret and sparing both of us from a loveless match.

*(A commotion offstage. SMERALDINA bursts in and strikes a pose. The GUARDS are caught off-guard. They start to perform their impressive entrance business but trail off awkwardly, since SMERALDINA has already entered. Beat. SMERALDINA advances making ridiculous and over-the-top curtsies and gestures, fanning herself vigorously.)*

DERAMO: And who are you? Please be seated. *(Aside)* She looks just like my butler's sister.

SMERALDINA: *(Seating herself with a flourish)* It is I, my lord, Smeraldina, sister to Brighella. We come from a high lineage, but, alas, poor fortune has lowered us to this state. But poverty can never defile *true* gentility.

*(SMERALDINA fans herself tragically, shedding feathers in every direction; much batting of eyelashes The STATUE shakes with silent laughter.)*

*(DERAMO, noting the STATUE's reaction:)*

DERAMO: Most certainly. *(Clearly there's no point in beating around the bush)* Tell me, my lady—do you love me?

SMERALDINA: *(Sighing loudly)* Oh! ...Oh! ...You tyrant, you fiend, what kind of question is that? I have been conquered by you.

*(More sighing from SMERALDINA. The STATUE laughs even harder than before.)*

DERAMO: *(Looking at the STATUE)* I see. Tell me more. If I were to choose you for my bride, and I died before you, would it grieve you?

SMERALDINA: Oh, you cruel thing! What are you saying? If you were not a vicious tiger in human form, you wouldn't say such things. Alas, I feel faint just thinking about the pain.

*(SMERALDINA pretends to faint. STATUE laughs with silent hysteria.)*

DERAMO: *(Seeing STATUE's reaction)* Oh, what a shame! Now I must call for servants to carry away this sensitive lady.

SMERALDINA: *(Hearing this, quickly comes to)* Where am I? What happened?

DERAMO: Lady, your affection is too great. Just one final question. Have you been married before? Or promised yourself to another?

SMERALDINA: Oh, no, no, no! I am but a tender, sweet young thing who has never even been kissed.

(SMERALDINA *fans herself vigorously. The* STATUE *is laughing enormously, making bizarre faces with its mouth wide open.)*

DERAMO: *(Sees the* STATUE *convulsing)* That's enough, my lady. You may go. I promise you that of all the women who have appeared before me, no one has pleased me as much as you have. Go, now. I will announce my decision later.

(SMERALDINA *continues to lounge, fan herself, bat eyelashes, and so on.)*

DERAMO: Please depart.

SMERALDINA: *(Rising happily)* Oh, my lord, I am a sea of affection, I am overwhelmed by the sweetest and most tender sentiments. Oh, how I yearn for our wedding day—then you will know just how much I love you! Farewell! *(Aside)* I've done it! I've won! I'm going to be queen!

(SMERALDINA *heads for the exit, with many affected curtsies and huge sighs, turning to glance back at* DERAMO, *as she does.)*

*(The* GUARDS *perform their exit business as* SMERALDINA *leaves.* DERAMO *relaxes.* SMERALDINA *bursts back in, blows kisses and exits again;* GUARDS *attempt to perform entrance and exit business simultaneously; they subside awkwardly. A moment of embarrassment.)*

DERAMO: *(To the* STATUE) Oh, dear statue, what pleasure you give me with your laugh! *(Looking toward the door)* And now it is Angela's turn. I hope… Foolish desire! After all this time, it is hard to hope. And yet, I still hope. Why am I hesitating? Statue, reveal the truth!

*(The* GUARDS *perform their entrance business.* ANGELA
*enters.* DERAMO *and* ANGELA *stand, staring at each other.
A long moment. The* GUARDS *look at each other; they repeat
their entrance business, startling* DERAMO *and* ANGELA *out
of their reverie.)*

DERAMO: Angela. *(Aside)* This is harder than I thought
it would be.

ANGELA: *(Simply)* Here I am, my king, by your order.
Whether it is just or not, I do not know.

DERAMO: Angela, please sit; I am never unjust.

ANGELA: You are a king. Who could have the courage
to tell you openly if your orders are unjust?

DERAMO: Angela has never lacked courage, and hardly
seems to lack courage now. But even if she did, I would
wish her to be given every liberty in front of her king.
Speak frankly. I will not take offence.

ANGELA: What kind of justice is it, Sire, to force
unhappy girls to present themselves in this secret
room, and to compete to be the wife of a king? Young
women daring to hope and then rejected, leaving
full of shame and misery. What kind of justice is it
for me, brought here, despite the pleas of my poor
father? A father who hoped his daughter might escape
the embarrassment of so many unfortunate women,
who have suffered in the face of your greatness, your
wisdom, or (could it be) your whims? My king—
Deramo—I speak not for my own sake, but for the
poor women who sadly wait outside this room.
Release them. Let me be the last to suffer the pain and
embarrassment of your rejection. My king, pardon me;
you gave me liberty to speak, and liberty I have taken.

DERAMO: I pardon you, Angela—and I thank you. Your
criticism is just. But if you knew my sad story, you
would understand my actions. In the past, I sought for

a sincere woman who would love me, who would love me until death, who would love me even if I didn't wear a crown; and I never found her. Only my duty to provide an heir to the throne forces me to try again today, and I am afraid my search will be in vain.

ANGELA: And what assures you, sire, that none of the women who have come before were sincere?

DERAMO: I am certain. I promise you, though I cannot tell you how I know.

ANGELA: As you wish, my king.

DERAMO: Angela. We have known each other for a long time. Please trust me.

(ANGELA *and* DERAMO *sit for a moment.*)

DERAMO: Angela—do you love me?

(*Another moment.*)

ANGELA: I wish to heaven that I did not love you, so that this didn't cause me so much pain.

(DERAMO *looks at the statue, which doesn't move:*)

DERAMO: *(Aside)* Not even a smile from the statue! *(A final doubt)* Angela, do you speak the truth? If you do not truly love me—or, if you love another—if your heart holds any secrets—please tell me, Angela, for pity's sake.

ANGELA: Oh, please, Deramo, end this. What honor can you find in this barbaric exercise? Why torment an unhappy woman? I can't bear it. I won't bear it. You may be my king, but my heart can only take so much.

(DERAMO *looks, as before at the* STATUE, *which doesn't move:*)

DERAMO: It is over. I am sorry for this ordeal, Angela. I love you so dearly and I could not bear it if you betrayed me—I would die of heartache.

ANGELA: Is this a trick?

DERAMO: No, Angela, forgive me. I should have trusted my heart. And yours. *(He takes her hands.)* Please, forgive me.

ANGELA: I don't know what to think.

DERAMO: My dear Angela, think that I love you, think that I honor your beautiful spirit, think you are worthy of a far greater monarch than I. *(A breath for courage)* Angela, will you share your life with me?

ANGELA: Deramo, I will.

*(A kiss)*

*(The GUARDS become verklempt.)*

DERAMO: Ministers, guards, enter, enter! Let the people rejoice! I have discovered a woman who loves me, and will love me forever, to the delight of my heart!

*(The GUARDS perform their entrance business, this time ending it with a cheer. TARTAGLIA, PANTALONE, CLARISSA, LEANDER, SMERALDINA, and BRIGHELLA enter.)*

DERAMO: Ministers, enter: I have found my partner at last. I have chosen Angela, and she has chosen me.

*(Big reactions from everyone—delight, relief, horror, as appropriate. TRUFFALDINO pops up out of a trapdoor in a vom and, pointing at SMERALDINA, lets out a derisive laugh.)*[7]

*(SMERALDINA proclaims that she still loves him—while standing on the pouffe so as to better proclaim her love. Explains that the only reason she went before the king was because BRIGHELLA made her.)*

BRIGHELLA: What?!

7       SMERALDINA *and* TRUFFALDINO's *exchange is improvised.*

(TRUFFALDINO *says that he detests her for having presented herself to the king against his wishes. He doesn't want another man's cast-off as a wife.*)

(SMERALDINA *protests; Pookie, my love for you is still strong, etc.*)

(TRUFFALDINO *exclaims that he never wants to see her again.*)

(TRUFFALDINO *disappears back into the vom platform.* SMERALDINA *collapses dramatically on the pouffe.*)

SMERALDINA: Noooooooooooo!

(*An exasperated* BRIGHELLA *rolls the pouffe with the prostrate* SMERALDINA *offstage.*)

(*A beat*)

PANTALONE: My daughter, Majesty?

DERAMO: Yes, your daughter, fortunate father!

TARTAGLIA: (*Aside*) Oh, tragedy! I feel like I'm dying! (*With affected joy*) Long live you both, Majesty! I rejoice! You could not have made a better choice. Angela, I congratulate you. Pantalone, I cannot express my joy. (*Aside*) The anger gnaws at my gut! Violence! Death! Revenge!

PANTALONE: (*Joins his daughter and embraces her*) Dear daughter, never forget your humble birth. If you will accept recommendations from your judicious, old father, if, before your wedding, our king will grant me two hours to advise you— But what am I saying? It all still seems impossible to me—

DERAMO: Hush, old friend.

(PANTALONE *steps back and* DERAMO *extends his hand to* ANGELA.)

DERAMO: Angela, here is my hand. With this hand, I give you my spirit and my eternal faith.

ANGELA: *(Taking his hand)* Deramo, here is my hand, and with this hand, I give you my spirit and my eternal faith.

*(A moment. LEANDER and CLARISSA are overcome; they draw close to each other and sniffle happily.)*

TARTAGLIA: *(Aside)* Oh, I'm dying of rage!

*(ANGELA and DERAMO lean in for a kiss, which TARTAGLIA interrupts)*

TARTAGLIA: But how is it, most beloved monarch, that you are so sure, after having rejected two thousand, seven hundred, and forty-eight damsels?

DERAMO: I will tell you. Five years ago I received from the magician Durandarte two great secrets, one of which is this

*(DERAMO gestures towards the STATUE; they all look.)*

DERAMO: and one other that I keep locked in my heart. This statue has a magic power—it laughs when it hears people lie. Thanks to its power, I know that of all the women who have appeared before me, Angela is the only one who sincerely and truly loves me. I have chosen Angela, because she has chosen me.

*(General amazement. CLARISSA looks guilty. PANTALONE peers at the STATUE curiously.)*

PANTALONE: Well, now, that's a heck of a thing!

TARTAGLIA: And this statue laughed at Clarissa! That means my daughter is a liar.

*(TARTAGLIA makes a move toward CLARISSA. ANGELA and LEANDER put themselves between CLARISSA and her father.)*

DERAMO: Hold! Clarissa is in love with another. The statue knew. Dear minister, be content. Your daughter has done nothing wrong.

TARTAGLIA: If you say so, your Majesty.

DERAMO: I do. My Angela, I love you dearly. And to prove that I trust you, I order that this infernal statue be demolished so I am never tempted to dishonor your faith and love by testing them.

*(The* STATUE *has a moment of panic, leaps off the platform, and runs out of the theatre.)*

*(Beat)*

DERAMO: Let the city rejoice! Let us celebrate together! Gather our friends for a festive hunt!

*(Exclamations of celebration and excitement. These people really like their hunts.)*

ANGELA: Who would have thought that a day begun in sorrow could end in such joy?

PANTALONE: It all seems like a dream to me!

LEANDER: Oh, Clarissa!

CLARISSA: Oh, Leander!

*(*DERAMO, ANGELA, PANTALONE, *and* LEANDER *exit.* TARTAGLIA *seizes* CLARISSA *as she attempts to exit.)*

TARTAGLIA: Cheat! Cheat! Cheat! Assassin! Because of you I have lost all of my happiness! By revealing your little crush on Leander, you've ruined us both at the same moment. May you be afflicted by boils! Cankers! Apoplexy!

CLARISSA: No, father; I revealed nothing, I swear; it was the statue that discovered my true feelings.

TARTAGLIA: Statue or no statue, feelings or no feelings, who gave you permission to fall in love with Leander? If you hadn't been in love, the statue wouldn't have laughed, you nit, you wretch, you…ninny!

CLARISSA: Oh, please, Father, don't curse me, please, consider this—since I was rejected today, you could console me by letting me marry Leander. You've always wanted me to marry well, and since Leander's sister is now queen, Leander herself will rise in rank and privilege!

TARTAGLIA: Listen, you minx— *(Aside)* My bile betrays me. If I want to revenge myself, I must hide my feelings. *(With affected sweetness)* Dearest daughter of mine, pay no attention to what I've said. I spoke hastily; it's all been a terrible shock. I had such high hopes. Bear with me, give me time, wait for my anger to pass. I will comfort you, but do not rush me. *(Aside)* Otherwise I'll lock you in your room for the rest of your days.

CLARISSA: Yes, father, yes, I understand. I am comforted.

TARTAGLIA: Fine, fine, fine, but go to your room now.

CLARISSA: Yes, father, but please, let me kiss you first.

TARTAGLIA: Yes, yes, yes, fine, fine, fine, kiss me...

*(CLARISSA kisses TARTAGLIA's cheek; he endures it.)*

TARTAGLIA: Now go away, let my anger subside a bit.

*(TARTAGLIA pushes CLARISSA offstage.)*

TARTAGLIA: Kisses? Kisses?! Kisses?!! All I want to do is shake you until your teeth rattle! I've lost everything! Everything! At this moment the married couple is sitting...talking...holding hands... *(He has fit of rage, stomping, flailing, etc.)* Oh, I'm dying! I am full of jealousy and hate and awful, awful feelings! My nerves are like a million little spiders stampeding up and down my spine! I can't bear it—my rage is a burning flame—I curse my daughter, Pantalone, the king, and that infernal statue! *(Gets himself under control)* Patience, Tartaglia, patience. I will bide my time—I will wait—until I find the right moment to take the most astonishing revenge that has ever been seen in the theatre!

(TARTAGLIA *strikes a suitably villainous pose, then makes a grand exit.*)

(CIGLIOTTI *enters and signals a scene change.* BRIGHELLA *enters and, grumbling under his breath, removes the statue's pedestal. The* GUARDS *march out. The stage is empty.*)

(CIGLIOTTI *whistles to the* PARROT, *which enters.*)

CIGLIOTTI: Mighty Durandarte, is this the entrance to the forest of Noname?

PARROT: Yes, Cigolotti—release me! Release me!

(CIGLIOTTI's *gesture sends the* PARROT *sweeping about the stage; it makes a wide circle then exits.*)

CIGLIOTTI: Farewell, Durandarte. Go and work your great portents! At [ten o'clock this evening] I'll see you in your former human state and we will raise a toast to good health, happiness, and peace for all humankind.

(CIGLIOTTI *snaps his fingers as he exits, signaling the music for intermission.*)

### END OF ACT ONE

# ACT TWO

## Scene 1

*(Setting: An open space, which* CIGLIOTTI *will transform into the Forest of Noname.)*

*(At rise:* CIGLIOTTI *enters; he snaps his fingers. The lights change, and branches swirl about him as giant* TREES *enter through the voms and the forest takes shape.* CIGLIOTTI *manipulates the entrances and exits of each character, pulling them onstage and sending them off, as if he controls invisible strings. He moves through the space, watching the action.)*

*(The* PARROT *flies through the space and exits.)*

*(*TRUFFALDINO *wanders in, looking for birds, he tries some of his bird whistles—warbling, a duck call, old-fashioned "awoogah" car horn; he exits.)*

*(Two* DEER*—both stags, one with a white mark on its forehead—enter the space, they look about, hear a noise, freeze, then dart offstage.)*

*(The* TREES *move in response to the passages of the* PARROT *and the* DEER, *but freeze when* TRUFFALDINO *enters. Throughout the act, the* TREES *will follow and react to the action occurring onstage, sometimes only facially, sometimes with their whole bodies.)*

(DERAMO *and* TARTAGLIA *enter with crossbows. The*
TREES *freeze.* CIGLIOTTI *checks to make sure the scene is set
properly, then exits.)*[8]

DERAMO: *(Surveying the scene)* This, Tartaglia, this is
where we'll wait.

TARTAGLIA: Yes, yes, yes, your Majesty; it's an
attractive place.

DERAMO: Some creature will surely pass this way—

(DERAMO *turns away from* TARTAGLIA, *who raises his
weapon and takes aim at his back. The* TREES *frantically
attempt to draw* DERAMO's *attention to* TARTAGLIA, *but he
does not see them.)*

DERAMO: —and then we will test our skill.

(DERAMO *turns back toward* TARTAGLIA, *who pretends to
have been doing warm-up calisthenics.)*

TARTAGLIA: Oh, certainly. *(Aside)* If he would only
stand still!

DERAMO: *(Strolling over to a new spot)* I remember seeing
many deer in this very spot.

(DERAMO *turns his back;* TARTAGLIA *aims his crossbow
at* DERAMO. *Again, the* TREES *attempt to signal* DERAMO,
*who doesn't see them.)*

(DERAMO *turns back toward* TARTAGLIA, *who again
awkwardly covers up what he's been doing.)*

TARTAGLIA: Of course, of course. I remember. *(Aside)*
Soon Angela—and the kingdom—will be mine!

DERAMO: Where could the other hunters be?

8       *ACT TWO costume choices were designed to facilitate*
DERAMO *and* TARTAGLIA's *magical transformation that occurs
later in the scene. Both actors wore the same pants, with different
top coats.* DERAMO *wore glasses and a tall top hat with a crown
circlet around its base.* TARTAGLIA *also wore a shorter top hat and
a cloak.*

*(As* DERAMO *turns his back, the business with the crossbow is repeated. This time, a* TREE *manages to tap* DERAMO *on the head, causing him to turn back around before* TARTAGLIA *can get in a shot.)*

TARTAGLIA: Oh, Sire, the others are far away. *(Aside)* Gah! Just one moment longer!

DERAMO: *(Observing his muttering)* Dear Tartaglia, you seem very melancholy. Friend, is there something in your heart that grieves you? I can't bear seeing you so sad. You have always been such a comfort to me. Let us sit here and talk as friends. *(He sits under a* TREE.*)*

TARTAGLIA: *(Aside)* I'll have to wait for a better time. *(To* DERAMO*)* Why, why, why, your Majesty, there isn't anything wrong at all.

DERAMO: No, Tartaglia, there is. I can see that your heart is troubled. Please, unburden yourself, sit down; remember that I am your friend and that I love you dearly.

*(*TARTAGLIA *sits under another* TREE; *the* TREE *is not pleased to have him there.)*

TARTAGLIA: *(Aside)* I will mix lies with truth, so that he does not suspect me. *(To* DERAMO*)* Sire, I can no longer keep silent. My mortification is without measure.

DERAMO: From what cause, faithful minister? Tell me what has displeased you, so I may avenge you, or seek to justify my actions.

TARTAGLIA: Sire, for years I have served you with the greatest faithfulness. How many times have I exposed myself to danger during bloody battles? Battles caused by your rejection of princesses! For you, I have shed my blood and risked my life. If only I had died before now, so I might have been spared the mortification of being wounded by you, whom I love more than I love myself.

(TARTAGLIA *pretends to weep. Loudly. The* TREES *wince.*)

DERAMO: How have I offended you? Dearest minister, how? Tell me, Tartaglia.

(TARTAGLIA *pretends to be too emotional to speak.*)

DERAMO: Come, Tartaglia, explain yourself.

TARTAGLIA: For five years—five! —you have possessed the secrets of the magician Durandarte. And yet you did not reveal them to me, your faithful minister, who most merits your trust. Perhaps you were right not to do so, but to force my poor daughter to face the judgment of that wretched statue—its laughter will ring forever in my ears, reminding me that I am unworthy of your deepest confidence.

(*Great histrionic weeping from* TARTAGLIA. *The* TREES *are variously appalled, disgusted, and generally displeased.*)

DERAMO: Tartaglia, my most faithful minister, I was wrong not to trust you. Your complaints are just. How can I redeem this wrong and show you that I trust you more than any of my other friends?

(TARTAGLIA *renews his histrionic performance. Weeping. So much weeping. The* TREES *roll their eyes.* DERAMO *attempts to console* TARTAGLIA *with an awkward pat on the shoulder. Gets an idea:*)

DERAMO: Listen, my friend, I will share with you the greatest and most terrible secret that was left to me by that powerful magician.

(TARTAGLIA'*s attention is caught. He stops weeping. The* TREES *are also interested.*)

DERAMO: It is in the form of a spell, a spell so powerful that I never let it out of my keeping. (*He takes a small piece of paper out of his coat pocket.*) Listen, my friend, to its terrifying power.

(TARTAGLIA—*and the* TREES—*lean in to better hear this exciting new information.)*

DERAMO: If you recite this verse over a lifeless body— whether it be the body of an animal or of a person—the spell will cause you to trade bodies. Your spirit will magically pass into the dead body and reanimate it, leaving your body lifeless on the ground.

TARTAGLIA: What? What? What? If I recite this verse over…a dead donkey, say, I will then enter into the donkey and it will resurrect itself, leaving my body dead on the ground, and me with the advantage of remaining a donkey for the rest of my days. Oh, Majesty, why must you mock me?

DERAMO: Wait, Tartaglia. When you no longer wish to inhabit the borrowed body, return to your corpse and stand over it. Speak the same verse and your spirit will return to your own body, returning you to life, and the other to death. *(He rises.)* Through the power of this magic verse, I have discovered hidden rebellions, secret traitors, and enormous misdeeds, allowing me to keep this realm safe from evildoers. And now I will share it with you.

*(Gives* TARTAGLIA *the paper with the magic verse. The* TREES *are alarmed.)*

DERAMO: Memorize it, and no longer say that I do not trust and respect you, my friend.

*(*DERAMO *embraces* TARTAGLIA*)*

TARTAGLIA: *(Clutching the paper with the magic verse. Aside)* This may allow me to revenge myself and to claim my Angela! *(To* DERAMO*)* My king, forgive me for what I said before. This is a great secret, a great sign of your generous confidence. Please, let me… *(He begins to kneel.)*

DERAMO: Rise, dear friend. Learn the great spell by heart, and let us search for a better hunting grounds, since we haven't seen a single creature pass this way.

(DERAMO *exits.* TARTAGLIA *opens the paper and attempts to read the spell out loud, stumbling over the words.*)

TARTAGLIA: "Cra cra, trif traf, scott flott naomi!" Gah! Stupid spell! *(To the audience)* Never mind! It may be difficult to say, but could still serve me well! *(He exits, muttering, never quite getting the words of the verse right.)*

*(The voices of hunters—*PANTALONE, BRIGHELLA, *and* LEANDER—*are heard offstage, along with the sound of horns.)*

*(A* BEAR *enters, followed by the hunters, who are all armed with crossbows.* BRIGHELLA *fires at the bear, which flees up the stairs of the aisle to the upper concourse. The* TREES, *throughout this scene, are on the side of the* BEAR.)

BRIGHELLA: Missed completely! Your turn, Minister!

PANTALONE: You nincompoop, get out of my way! My turn!

*(*PANTALONE *fires at the bear, misses. The* BEAR *runs around the concourse.)*

BRIGHELLA: Missed! It's getting further away, Minister!

PANTALONE: I sneezed! Your turn, daughter! The bear is still within range! Your turn!

LEANDER: My shot! My shot!

*(*LEANDER *fires and misses.* BEAR *changes direction, runs the opposite way around the concourse.)*

PANTALONE: He's escaping, the devil take him!

*(The* BEAR *exits the concourse.)*

LEANDER: Hurry, Brighella! Hurry!

*(*BRIGHELLA *fires. There is a "yipe" from offstage.)*

PANTALONE: You idiot! You've nicked one of the dogs!

LEANDER: To the mountain! Hurry!

(LEANDER *charges up the stairs to the concourse.)*

BRIGHELLA: To the mountain! I'll circle around him! *(He charges up the stairs to the concourse.)*

PANTALONE: To the mountain! And stay alert as you follow!

(PANTALONE *starts up the stairs to the concourse more slowly—old knees aren't quite up to charging.)*

PANTALONE: Hurry, hurry!

*(The* BEAR *runs out of a vom.* PANTALONE, *partway up the stairs, sees him and heads back down the stairs to follow the bear.)*

PANTALONE: The bear! The bear!

*(The* BEAR *crosses the stage and disappears into another vom.)*

(LEANDER *and* BRIGHELLA *run out of the same vom that the* BEAR *entered from. They charge past* PANTALONE, *who is making his way after the* BEAR, *cross the stage, and disappear into the vom the bear went into.)*

*(Just as* PANTALONE *is about to exit the stage in pursuit, the* BEAR *runs out of a different vom, crosses the stage, and disappears.)*

(LEANDER *and* BRIGHELLA *run out of the vom the bear came from, cross the stage, and disappear.* PANTALONE *changes directions and heads toward the vom that the bear and hunters have run into.)*

*(Just as* PANTALONE *reaches the vom,* LEANDER *and* BRIGHELLA, *yelling wildly, run back out of the vom, followed by the* BEAR. *They sweep* PANTALONE *up, race across the stage, and frantically exit—pursued by* BEAR.)*

*(Beat)*

*(The* DEER *enter the space, explore their surroundings. The* TREES *hear* DERAMO *and* TARTAGLIA *returning and warn the deer, who exit.)*

*(*DERAMO *and* TARTAGLIA *reenter.)*

DERAMO: I thought I heard the other hunters but there's no one here.

TARTAGLIA: With all that hullaballoo, I thought we'd find a dead rhinoceros at least!

DERAMO: *(Peering into the distance)* Tartaglia, I see two stags heading this way. Quick, let us hide!

*(*DERAMO *and* TARTAGLIA *hide themselves on opposite sides of the stage.)*

*(The* DEER *reenter.)*

*(The following happens in a slow, dreamlike fashion:* DERAMO *rises from his hiding place, raises his crossbow, and kills one of the* DEER. TARTAGLIA *rises from his hiding place, raises his crossbow, kills the other* DEER.)*

*(*DERAMO *and* TARTAGLIA, *back in real time, cross to examine the dead* DEER.)*

TARTAGLIA: Bravo, bravo, bravissimo, Majesty!

DERAMO: Both were noble beasts.

TARTAGLIA: *(Aside)* Ah, I have the most wonderful idea! If it succeeds, I will revenge my injury! And Angela will be mine! *(To* DERAMO) My, my, my king, these stags are dead—

DERAMO: Without a doubt. They are no longer moving.

TARTAGLIA: Since we are alone and all the other hunters are far away, could we not try an experiment with the magic verse, and, passing into the bodies of these stags, amuse ourselves by going over that hill to see the beautiful view? Just, just, just for a moment.

Such a marvel seems impossible to me; I have such a longing to try it.

DERAMO: A splendid idea, Tartaglia! Then you will see that I have not lied to you. Go, stand above one of the stags, speak the magic verse, and you will be transported into its body.

TARTAGLIA: *(Pulls back; laughing nervously)* Heh, heh, ha, ha—Majesty, I'm not sure I understand—heh, heh, ha, ha—I'm sure you're joking—heh, heh…

DERAMO: I understand—it must seem impossible that what I say is true. I will go first, so you may see how it is done. Then repeat the spell over the body of the other stag, and follow me.

*(DERAMO stands above the DEER with the white mark on its forehead and speaks the magic verse. DERAMO's spirit leaves his body and enters the body of the DEER, which rises, returning to life. The DEER turns its head toward TARTAGLIA, pauses a moment, then exits. DERAMO's body remains on the ground.)*[9]

TARTAGLIA: *(As DERAMO)* Astonishing! *(Gently nudges the body)* Courage, Tartaglia, soon you will be revenged and happy! I will steal the body of the king, take over his kingdom, and make Angela my own. Let's lose no more time.

*(TARTAGLIA stands over the body of DERAMO, but as he is about to speak the verse, he hears the clamor of horns and hunters.)*

*(The BEAR runs on, followed by PANTALONE, LEANDER, and BRIGHELLA, who are holding their crossbows.*

9        *How we did it: this was the easiest of the "dreamscape" transformations—after speaking the verse, the actor playing DERAMO sank slowly down as the actor playing the DEER rose at the same time and at the same speed. Each actor moved in a clockwise direction, which helped give the impression that a single transformative event was occurring.*

TARTAGLIA *hides behind a* TREE, *who is not happy about it.*
*The* BEAR *exits, followed by the hunters.)*

*(*TARTAGLIA *stands over the body of the king and starts to*
*speak the verse "Cra, cra, etc.")*

*(The* BEAR *runs on again, followed by* PANTALONE,
LEANDER, *and* BRIGHELLA. TARTAGLIA *hides again. The*
BEAR *exits, followed by the hunters.)*

*(*TARTAGLIA *stands over the body of the king. Starts to*
*speak. Stops, looks to see if anyone is coming. Then speaks*
*the verse "Cra, cra, etc." The spell exchanges* DERAMO *and*
TARTAGLIA's *bodies.)*[10]

*(*TARTAGLIA *realizes that he is now in the body of the king.*
*He stands over his enemy.)*

TARTAGLIA: *(As* DERAMO. *Triumphantly)* Let Deramo—

*(*PANTALONE, LEANDER, *and* BRIGHELLA *run across the*
*stage pursued by the* BEAR—*who now holds one of the*
*crossbows.* TARTAGLIA *hides. Hunters and* BEAR *exit.*
TARTAGLIA *stomps back over to his old body, and resumes*
*gloating.)*

TARTAGLIA: Let Deramo— *(Stops, quick check—no one's*
*coming)* Let Deramo remain in misery! I am now king—
the kingdom and Angela will be mine! *(Speaking to his*
*dead body)* And you, my body, must go, so that the king
cannot make use of you and will remain trapped in

10      *How we did it: as with all the transformations, we*
*used slow, dreamlike choreography. Here, the actors playing*
TARTAGLIA *and* DERAMO *circled each other while trading*
*costume pieces [coats, hats, glasses, etc.]. At the end of the*
*transformation, the actor playing* TARTAGLIA *was wearing*
DERAMO's *outer costume pieces—the conceit was that the actor*
*playing* TARTAGLIA *now resembled* DERAMO, *which he supported*
*by assuming* DERAMO's *physical and vocal mannerisms when in*
*the company of other characters. The actor playing* DERAMO, *after*
*changing into* TARTAGLIA's *costume, sank back to the ground,*
*with his face obscured by* TARTAGLIA's *cloak.*

the body of that stag. Into the river with you, unhappy body of Tartaglia! Your concerns are no longer mine.

(TARTAGLIA *casts his body offstage; the* TREES *register their distress.*)[11]

(*Voices are heard offstage. The returning hunters are arguing about who should be blamed for the bear-hunting debacle.*)

TARTAGLIA: *(As* DERAMO. *To the audience)* Here come the other hunters. Now I must appear grave. The stag that houses the spirit of Deramo must be pursued and killed! Once that stag is dead, I will have nothing left to fear.

(*Upon entering, the hunters bow to the supposed king, who stands with affected haughtiness. When speaking to other characters,* TARTAGLIA's *voice and physical mannerisms are those of* DERAMO's, *or rather, an over-the-top caricature of* DERAMO. *When* TARTAGLIA *speaks to the audience, he drops back into the vocal and physical characteristics of* TARTAGLIA. *When upset,* TARTAGLIA's *performance of* DERAMO *starts to slip.*)

TARTAGLIA: *(As* DERAMO*)* Hurry, ministers, hurry. Two stags appeared in this place; one lies here. The other has a white mark on its forehead—it went off that way. Whoever slays or captures the stag with the white mark will have from me whatever favor they choose to ask. Follow me!

(TARTAGLIA-*as*-DERAMO *exits*)

PANTALONE: Onward nimble youths! Obey your Majesty. (*He exits.*)

11      *How we did it: rather than having one actor pick the other up,* TARTAGLIA *reached down and grasped* DERAMO's *wrist. This allowed* DERAMO *to assist in the choreography;* DERAMO *rose as* TARTAGLIA *pulled him up and spun him offstage.*

LEANDER: If I find the stag, I'll ask to marry Clarissa! *(He exits.)*

BRIGHELLA: Come on, let's go! Or it'll be just like that bear! *(He exits.)*

*(A great noise from offstage—horns and voices shouting, "There he is! There he is!" While everyone is offstage shouting and shooting, the* DEER *enters, looks about, grazes or scratches, looks about calmly again, then trots offstage. The hunters rush back on, firing their crossbows in every direction.)*

PANTALONE: My shot! *(Shoots and misses)*

LEANDER: My shot! *(Shoots and misses)*

BRIGHELLA: My shot! *(Shoots and misses)*

TARTAGLIA: *(As* DERAMO*)* Oh, you idiots!

*(A frail* OLD MAN *enters; his body is bent over; a hood obscures his face. He is played by the same actor who plays* DERAMO.*)*

TARTAGLIA: *(As* DERAMO. *To the* OLD MAN*)* You, old man, did you see which way that deer went? The one that passed this way?

OLD MAN: No, I didn't see a deer.

TARTAGLIA: *(As* DERAMO*)* You didn't see it? How could you not see it? *(With the utmost fury)* I will not be lied to! I am your king, I demand the truth!

*(*TARTAGLIA *aims his crossbow at the* OLD MAN *and advances on him.)*

OLD MAN: *(Clutching his heart)* I...arrrr... *(He collapses, dead)*

*(*LEANDER, BRIGHELLA, *and* PANTALONE, *horrified, start to move toward the* OLD MAN.*)*

TARTAGLIA: *(As* DERAMO*)* Stop! Leave him! I want that deer! Take one step and you're next!

PANTALONE: *(Aside)* Has my king lost his mind?

LEANDER: *(Aside)* He can't be serious!

BRIGHELLA: *(Aside)* Well, that's it, I'm out of here.

PANTALONE: Majesty, I don't understand—are you unwell?

TARTAGLIA: *(As* DERAMO*)* Do not annoy me—I know how to rid myself of those who serve no purpose. Surround this wood—I want that deer! Make it known to all—whoever produces the stag with the white mark on his forehead will receive a thousand coins of gold! *(Makes a show of looking around)* Now, where is Tartaglia?

PANTALONE: *(Aside)* What has happened to my king? I don't recognize him anymore.

TARTAGLIA: *(As* DERAMO*)* Where is Tartaglia, I say?

PANTALONE: Your majesty, Tartaglia was with you.

TARTAGLIA: *(As* DERAMO*)* True, but I lost sight of him a long time ago.

LEANDER: He may have returned to the palace. It's nearby and he knows the way.

TARTAGLIA: *(As* DERAMO*)* Yes, yes, yes, but I know that he is hated because I love him, and I don't want some dastardly accident to befall him. Leave that old wretch and bring the stag. I wish to present it to my dear Angela, whom I cannot wait to embrace.

*(*TARTAGLIA-*as-*DERAMO *exits)*

PANTALONE: *(To* LEANDER *and* BRIGHELLA*)*

Let us also go. *(Aside)* This is appalling! I would flee the country if I didn't have my children to protect.

*(*PANTALONE *exits.* LEANDER *and* BRIGHELLA *gather up the dead* DEER.*)*[12]

12    *How we did it: in this dreamscape,* BRIGHELLA *and*

LEANDER: Brighella, if I find that other stag, I can ask for permission to marry Clarissa!

BRIGHELLA: Heaven spare me from those with their heads full of love, it's all they can think about!

*(They exit. The other* DEER—*the one housing the spirit of* DERAMO—*enters. We hear the voice of* DERAMO; *the actor playing the* DEER *physically echoes his thoughts.)*

DERAMO: *(Voice)* Oh, Jove, I thank you for saving me from cruel danger! But what have I become! A creature pursued by hunters and dogs, exposed to the winds, and rain, and tempests. But my greatest pain is the thought of my Angela, at the mercy of the traitor. I cannot bear it. *(Sees the body of the* OLD MAN*)* But who is this poor soul! *(Sees that the* OLD MAN *is dead)* His body can serve him no longer. Perhaps with his help I can return home to my wife.

*(The* DEER *stands over the body of the* OLD MAN; *we hear* DERAMO's *voice recite the verse, "Cra, cra, etc.")*

*(The* DEER *sinks to the ground and the* OLD MAN *rises.)*

DERAMO: *(As* OLD MAN*)* Thank the heavens, I am again in a human body. *(Looks at his hands and touches his face)* But—am I Deramo? In such a body? Cruel minister, I should not have trusted you. Oh, Angela! I must get to court and find my wife… *(He stops.)* But how will I make her believe that I am her Deramo, if the traitorous Tartaglia has my body? And how could she love me in this form—so feeble and weak? Tired limbs, take courage. Angela is wise and good and true. Heaven—do not abandon me!

---

LEANDER *detached the antlered headdress from the actor playing the* DEER, *who was lying on the ground; as they lifted the headdress, the actor rose up with it.* BRIGHELLA *and* LEANDER *then lifted the headdress high, and the actor slowly walked out from underneath it and left the stage.*

(DERAMO-*as*-OLD MAN *exits, as the* PARROT *flies on, tries a couple of different perches, gives an impertinent squawk to the audience, and finds a place to settle.)*

(TRUFFALDINO *enters with a birdcage and a large bag that contains an assortment of bird-catching equipment. He looks about and decides that the place is suitable for catching birds.)*[13]

*(Bird sounds from one of the* TREES. TRUFFALDINO *chooses a butterfly net from his bag and attempts to catch the bird. Comic business.)*

*(Bird sounds from another* TREE. TRUFFALDINO *chooses a larger net from the bag. Attempts to catch bird. Comic business.)*

*(Bird sounds from third* TREE. TRUFFALDINO *dumps contents of his bag: various ridiculous items, including— but not limited to—an old-fashioned fumigator, a large loaf of bread, and a cat-carrier.* TRUFFALDINO *takes the fumigator and sneaks up on the third* TREE. *Vigorous spraying with the fumigator. There is the sound of a "thud."* TRUFFALDINO *mimes scooping up a small bird and places it carefully in the cat-carrier.)*

PARROT: Truffaldino.

(TRUFFALDINO *is amazed and terrified. He has no idea who is speaking.)*

PARROT: Truffaldino.

(TRUFFALDINO *looks around, sees the dead stag; completely freaks out believing that it was the dead stag that was calling his name. He tries to gather up all his things at one time.)*

PARROT: Truffaldino, do not be afraid.

13    *This bird-catching business was mimed and improvised, as in Gozzi's original. It's a lot of fun, but if you're running long, you can cut to* TRUFFALDINO'*s exchange with the* PARROT.

(TRUFFALDINO *drops all his things with a crash. He determines that the voice is not coming from the location of the dead stag. Suspects that it is the* PARROT.)

TRUFFALDINO: Attempts to speak to the PARROT, beginning with the usual words that one uses when addressing a magic parrot, "Oh, Royal Parrot, etc."

PARROT: Take me to court, to the queen.

TRUFFALDINO: To court? To the queen?

PARROT: Yes, yes, you will be rich, rich, rich. Look!

(*A paper falls from the sky.* TRUFFALDINO *grabs it.*)

TRUFFALDINO: (*Reads out loud*) "Whosoever finds a stag with a white mark on its forehead and brings it to the king will earn a reward of a thousand gold pieces. Signed, the King."

(TRUFFALDINO *checks the dead stag and discovers that it has a white mark on its forehead.*)

(TRUFFALDINO *happily runs to the* PARROT *and coaxes it into the birdcage.[14] Attempts to gather everything up—the deer, the cage, the net, etc. Bundles everything offstage except the deer.*)

PARROT: (*From offstage*) Truffaldino! Don't forget the deer!

(*A crash from offstage as* TRUFFALDINO *drops everything he's carrying.* TRUFFALDINO *comes back onstage. Attempts to lift and carry the* DEER *by himself. Fails.*)

(CIGLIOTTI *comes on, ready to orchestrate a scene change. Starts to do so, but is interrupted by* TRUFFALDINO, *who badgers him into helping him with the* DEER.[15] *They exit.*)

14      *Depending on your* PARROT *staging choices,* TRUFFALDINO *could also coax the* PARROT *into his bird-catching net or onto a perch. In a pinch, the* PARROT *can just follow him offstage.*
15      *How we did it: rather than hauling the* DEER *offstage, we echoed the dreamscape choreography that* LEANDER *and* BRIGHELLA *used with the other* DEER *(see note 12).*

*(End of scene)*

## Scene 2

*(A brief interlude)*

*(The* OLD MAN *enters the forest.* CIGLIOTTI *reenters and snaps his fingers. The forest begins to shift as the* OLD MAN *moves through it, with the* TREES *uprooting themselves and traveling offstage. The forest disappears and the* OLD MAN *is left alone in the space. A moment of vulnerability, alone in the empty space. Then the* OLD MAN *gathers his courage and exits.)*

*(*CIGLIOTTI *watches him go and then speaks to the audience.)*[16]

CIGLIOTTI: Hello again. Well. Things have a taken a bit of a dark turn, haven't they? Sorry about that. Listen, we can stop here, if it's all getting a little too scary. I mean, after all, we're supposed to be showing you a "magical comedy for all ages," and, you know, there's certainly been lots of magic, but what's going to happen to Angela, and Deramo, and our other friends, right? Not to mention the kingdom. Yikes. So much for comedy!

*(*BRIGHELLA *pokes his head out of a vom.)*

BRIGHELLA: *(In a stage whisper)* Cigolotti! What are you doing?

CIGLIOTTI: *("Excuse me a moment" gesture to audience)* I just want to let them to know that everything works out. You know, because some of them *(Indicating specific audience members)* might really be worried.

16      *This exchange between* CIGLIOTTI *and* BRIGHELLA *was necessary in the original production in order to facilitate costume changes for five* TREES *and a* DEER. *It can be cut if you don't use* TREES, *or don't need the* TREES *to change into the* GUARDS. *It was a fun moment, though.*

BRIGHELLA: *(Whispering as before)* That's ridiculous, this isn't supposed to be some kind of Brechtian fable! Just let them enjoy the story!

CIGLIOTTI: *(To the audience)* Well, if you *do* want to keep going, just remember that the darkest hour is right before the dawn, and that just when things seem helpless—

BRIGHELLA: You are *such* a control freak!

CIGLIOTTI: Takes one to know one!

*(BRIGHELLA starts to respond. We hear GUARDS preparing to enter.)*

BRIGHELLA: Ack! Places! *(He darts offstage.)*

CIGLIOTTI: *(To the audience)* Oops, I have to go. Hang in there. Hold tight to each other. We'll get through this.

*(CIGLIOTTI exits.)*

*(Three GUARDS march on and take up their positions—we are back at court.)*

*(End of scene)*

## Scene 3

*(TARTAGLIA, who has added a short sword to his costume, rushes on after ANGELA. His attempts to imitate DERAMO are ridiculous and clumsy.)*

ANGELA: Please, leave me in peace!

TARTAGLIA: *(As DERAMO)* My, my, my dearest, why have you changed? Where are your joyful spirits? I have followed you for an hour seeking your caresses, but you won't even deign to hold hands with me.

*(ANGELA stares at TARTAGLIA fixedly.)*

TARTAGLIA: *(Aside)* She stares at me! Does she guess the truth? No, that couldn't be. *(To ANGELA)* Come, come,

come, my dear, where is the faithful love you once
gave me?

ANGELA: *(Distressed, but firm)* Deramo, you are no
longer worthy of it. I don't know how, or why, but
I no longer recognize the man I loved. Something is
different.

TARTAGLIA: *(As DERAMO)* What? What? What? What
are you saying? Why?

ANGELA: I do not know. *(Studying him)* You have
the same handsome face that inspired my love. But
your sentiments, speech, thoughts, expressions,
movement—none of these are, or no longer seem to be,
those that captured my heart. My king, pardon me; it
was not your outer form that inspired my love. What
attracted me was your mind, your spirit, and your
beautiful soul. It's these that seem to have changed—I
don't understand what has happened.

TARTAGLIA: *(As DERAMO. Aside)* Curses! This is not
going as planned! *(Turning back to ANGELA)* Come,
come, come, don't cry, my beautiful Angela.

*(ANGELA is deeply distressed, but is not, in fact, crying.)*

ANGELA: Majesty, if you had behaved then as you are
behaving now, I would have said, "My lord, I do not
love you, and I do not wish to be your partner."

TARTAGLIA: *(As DERAMO)* Come, come, come, now,
these are baseless fixations. This is only an illness
caused by hysteria. The evil must be in your brain.
Dear one, let us call the doctors and they will
determine what is wrong with you.

ANGELA: Oh, of course, it's all in my mind! No, I am
certain that your ways are not those that they were
before. Please, let me go. Let me go to my rooms where
I can mourn the loss of the man that I loved. *(She exits.)*

TARTAGLIA: *(As* DERAMO. *Calling after her)* Yes, yes, yes, my dearest joy. I am quite certain that your illness will pass, and you will love me again. *(To the audience)* I must remain calm. I will use sweetness, blandishments, and pleading, and should they fail, I will turn to threats! I will show her that I am not to be trifled with! I am the king! I will destroy everything that annoys me and does not please me!

*(*CLARISSA *enters, distraught.)*

CLARISSA: Oh, my good king, justice, for pity's sake!

*(*CLARISSA *kneels before* TARTAGLIA.*)*

TARTAGLIA: *(As* DERAMO*)* Clarissa, what has happened?

CLARISSA: My poor father has disappeared in the woods, no one can find him. And there are signs of a struggle near the river. I fear something terrible has happened to him.

*(*TARTAGLIA, *gesturing for* CLARISSA *to rise:)*

TARTAGLIA: *(As* DERAMO*)* What? What? What is it you say? Who has dared to harm my faithful minister? Poor, poor, poor man. I feared for his safety! I knew that he was envied by his enemies! Reveal the names of the malefactors to me immediately.

CLARISSA: No one knows what has happened. No one knows who is to blame. All I know is that my heart is full of worry and sorrow, and I don't know where to turn.

*(*CLARISSA *weeps.* TARTAGLIA *is affected.)*

TARTAGLIA: *(As* DERAMO. *Aside)* I am actually moved. If only I could reveal my secret! *(Starts to embrace her, then draws back)* But I cannot trust her. *(To* CLARISSA*)* Hush, hush, hush, Clarissa; think of me as another father. There will be vengeance for my faithful friend! I will discover his fate and those responsible for it! But, but, but go now, my dear.

CLARISSA: I will obey you, my king. I thank you for your kindness.

(CLARISSA *exits.* LEANDER *enters at a run.*)

LEANDER: Sire, I have ominous tidings!

(PANTALONE *rushes in.*)

PANTALONE: Oh, Majesty…Majesty… Poor Tartaglia…

TARTAGLIA: *(As* DERAMO. *Fiercely)* I know everything! My poor minister! Most, most, most faithful friend! *(Pretends to be overcome)* Who brought this terrible news?

PANTALONE: Truffaldino, the court birdcatcher, your Majesty. He says there are signs of foul play by the banks of the river.

TARTAGLIA: *(As* DERAMO*)* You, there! Guards!

(GUARDS *enter.*)

TARTAGLIA: *(As* DERAMO*)* Let Truffaldino be imprisoned! Arrest everyone who was at the hunt today! Take Leander and Pantalone to the dungeon immediately! I will begin my investigation with these two.

LEANDER / PANTALONE: *(Speaking at the same time)* Me, Majesty? / Sir, this is madness!

TARTAGLIA: *(As* DERAMO. *To the* GUARDS*)* Obey me!

*(The* GUARDS *seize* LEANDER *and* PANTALONE*)*

TARTAGLIA: *(As* DERAMO*)* I know that you, Leander, loved his daughter, and I know that Tartaglia, my unfortunate friend, was reluctant to let you marry her! Perhaps you took matters into your own hands. *(To* PANTALONE*)* And you, old man, perhaps you wished to remove your rival, who was so dear to me. To the dungeon with you both—if you are innocent, I will absolve you.

LEANDER: Woe is me! All hope is lost.

(LEANDER *is taken off by the* GUARDS.)

PANTALONE: Heaven will defend my innocence!

(PANTALONE *is taken off by the* GUARDS.)

TARTAGLIA: (*As* DERAMO) That takes care of those who might threaten me! I just need to find that stag. Then no one can take the kingdom away from me. And Angela will be mine! She must!

(TARTAGLIA-*as*-DERAMO *exits*)

(*A transition: the* GUARDS *become the halls of the palace that* DERAMO-*as*-OLD MAN *must work his way through, looking for danger at every turn. He sinks down in exhaustion.* CIGLIOTTI *enters and directs the* GUARDS *to exit; he then exits as well.*)

DERAMO: (*As* OLD MAN) So weary! I can go no further. I am so tired I can barely stand. In this palace where I was king, I sneak about in the shadows, fearing everyone. I just wish to see my Angela, to explain— But, how could she possibly believe me? Who could blame her for not believing me?

(DERAMO *hides just as* ANGELA *enters.*)

ANGELA: What is happening! Tartaglia is believed dead? My father and my sister are in prison? What insanity is this? These tyrannies only confirm that my husband is different from what he was.

(TRUFFALDINO *enters with the* PARROT. *He is very pleased with himself.*)

TRUFFALDINO: Hello, Queen! You have come to pay your respects to me! No, sorry. *I* have come to pay my respects to *you*, and to give you this gift—

ANGELA: Oh, dear Truffaldino, I have too much on my mind to welcome your presents. Please leave me.

TRUFFALDINO: But I want to give you a parrot! The most intelligent parrot that has ever graduated from an institution of higher learning.

ANGELA: Truffaldino, please go, and take your parrot with you. Please. Don't bother me right now.

TRUFFALDINO: But your Majesty needs to understand— this is a magic parrot. A powerful parrot. The most clever and eloquent parrot in the world!

*(He presents the* PARROT *triumphantly.)*

TRUFFALDINO: Here you go, Parrot, here's your chance!

*(No answer from the* PARROT*)*

TRUFFALDINO: Don't be shy—it's the Queen!

*(Still no answer from the* PARROT*)*

TRUFFALDINO: Come on. Come on, Parrot.

*(*PARROT *turns away.)*

TRUFFALDINO: Listen, featherhead, this is your last chance!

ANGELA: Truffaldino, stop this nonsense or I'll call the guards!

TRUFFALDINO: So this is the reward I get for bringing you to the Queen? Avian traitor!

PARROT: Angela!

*(*ANGELA *starts in surprise. She gives the* PARROT *a sharp look. She starts to approach it.)*

*(*GUARDS *enter.)*

GUARD ONE: With your permission, my lady.

ANGELA: Oh, what now?

TRUFFALDINO: Not to worry, your Majesty. This person has obviously been sent by the king to give my reward— "1,000 gold coins for the stag with the white mark on its forehead." Thank you! *(He holds out his hand for the sack of gold.)*

GUARD ONE: The king commands that this man be thrown into the dungeon. He is a suspect, my lady, in the disappearance of Tartaglia. Come, rascal.

*(GUARD takes TRUFFALDINO by the arm.)*

TRUFFALDINO: Seriously?

ANGELA: Release him! This is insane!

GUARD ONE: I must obey my king. Come, you clown. This no time for your nonsense. *(To GUARD TWO)* Secure the parrot.

*(GUARD ONE begins to drag TRUFFALDINO away. GUARD TWO approaches the PARROT—it snaps at him and he backs off nervously.)*

*(GUARD marches TRUFFALDINO off.)*

TRUFFALDINO: *(As he's hauled off)* Stupid parrot! Stupid stag! Stupid me!

*(GUARD TWO timidly shoos the PARROT off in another direction.)*

PARROT: *(As it leaves the stage)* Angela! Magic! Secrets!

ANGELA: One catastrophe after another! Where will it all end? I must do something to help this poor fool— not to mention my father and my sister. This tyrant must be stopped! What can I do? Think, Angela, think!

DERAMO: *(As OLD MAN. Offstage)* My dearest, my life…

ANGELA: That is the voice of the king!

*(DERAMO-as-OLD MAN enters.)*

DERAMO: *(As OLD MAN. Raises a trembling hand toward ANGELA)* Do not be dismayed, my love, I beg you.

(DERAMO-*as*-OLD MAN *advances slowly.*)

ANGELA: Who are you? Who let you in? *(Aside)* The king must have sent him to spy on me! *(Advancing on* DERAMO-*as*-OLD MAN*)* Leave my room at once.

DERAMO: *(As* OLD MAN*)* For pity's sake, Angela, listen to me. Angela, I beg you, is there anything about me that you recognize?

ANGELA: Why would I recognize you? Who are you? Why are you here?

DERAMO: *(As* OLD MAN*)* Tell me, my love, do you not find the king to be suddenly and strangely different from who he was?

ANGELA: Who told you to ask me this?

DERAMO: *(As* OLD MAN*)* Do you remember when your Deramo destroyed the magic statue? Do you remember his words at the time? Five years ago I received from the magician Durandarte two great secrets, one of which is this, and one other that I keep locked in my heart."

ANGELA: Yes, those are his exact words. Where did you learn them?

DERAMO: *(As* OLD MAN*)* Do you remember, Angela, this very morning, before the hunt, when your Deramo teased you about your birthmark, saying that it marred your perfect beauty?

ANGELA: How could you know? How is it possible?

DERAMO: *(As* OLD MAN. *Summoning his strength)* Angela, know… Oh, Heaven, lend me your strength… Angela, know that I am your Deramo, trapped in a body that is not my own. My body, through the power of magic, now houses the spirit of the unfaithful Tartaglia. I trusted him too much, dear wife, and I grieve the disaster that has now fallen upon us, and our kingdom.

ANGELA: This is the voice of my love. You sound like my Deramo. I don't understand what has happened, but I can tell that it is you. Deramo.

(ANGELA *takes* DERAMO-*as*-OLD MAN *by the hand*)

DERAMO: (*As* OLD MAN) You love me still, my heart? How I love you, the rarest soul in all the world.

(DERAMO-*as*-OLD MAN *kisses* ANGELA'*s hand.*)

ANGELA: But how could so strange a metamorphosis be possible? Tartaglia is missing, Tartaglia is the king—what wonders! But I knew, I could tell, that the beautiful spirit of my husband had vanished. When your handsome body did not house your soul, I despised it. And now your traitorous minister vents his rage through tyranny. My unhappy father and my sister are already imprisoned. He threatens everyone. We must do something.

DERAMO: (*As* OLD MAN) If only Durandarte were here. How can we defeat magic without magic? I have no further secrets to aid me. Only this poor feeble body.

ANGELA: Magic… Secrets… (*Remembers where she's heard those words before*) Deramo—I have the strangest feeling about that parrot of Truffaldino's…

DERAMO: (*As* OLD MAN) Truffaldino's parrot?

ANGELA: Yes. But in the meantime, we need help. We need our friends and family. We must work together! Quick, come with me—trust me! We must find Clarissa…and that parrot!

(ANGELA *and* DERAMO-*as*-OLD MAN *exit, she supporting him.*)

(BRIGHELLA *runs on with* SMERALDINA *in hot pursuit.*)

BRIGHELLA: I'm fed up! Pull yourself together! I
have more important things on my mind than your
reputation. The king wants to put me in prison!

SMERALDINA: You traitor, your ambition was the cause
of my ruin! You wanted me to present myself to the
king and now Truffaldino doesn't want me anymore!
I have lost any opportunity for a good marriage, so
you had better start thinking of new ways to find me a
husband!

BRIGHELLA: Presenting yourself to the king your idea,
not mine! And you couldn't pull it off. You want me to
find you a husband? Forget it! Find him yourself!

SMERALDINA: Numskull! I've tried everything! I've
held hands with the footmen, made eyes at the waiters,
sighed at the guards, and winked at all the grooms
in the stables—but no one will even look at me! All
because of the king's rejection, which was entirely your
fault! Assassin of my reputation!

BRIGHELLA: Any assassination has come from your
crazy behavior! From your mania for finding a
husband! Now stop pestering me, you lunatic! I need
to hide.

(BRIGHELLA *bolts and escapes offstage.*)

SMERALDINA: Traitor! Pinhead! Nincompoop! (*She runs
after him.*)

(BRIGHELLA *runs in and out of voms, chased by an
increasing number of* GUARDS. SMERALDINA *chases the*
GUARDS. *Eventually, the* GUARDS *pounce on* BRIGHELLA,
*carry him off.*)

(ANGELA *enters, followed by* CLARISSA.)

CLARISSA: I don't understand. You want me to release
your sister and father from the dungeon? How? What
about the guards?

ANGELA: Tell them that Tartaglia has returned from the forest. Or that the king is in danger. Or that dragons are attacking. Use your wits, or a disguise, or anything else you can think of. Just help us!

CLARISSA: But what if I can't think of anything?

ANGELA: Clarissa, I know you, you can do this. You're stronger than you think.

CLARISSA: Oh, my dear friend, how did it come to this? Why do we have to face such dark times?

ANGELA: I don't know. But we have each other. We need to stick together, and we need to act.

CLARISSA: I'll do my best.

(ANGELA *and* CLARISSA *embrace and* CLARISSA *runs off as* DERAMO-*as*-OLD MAN *enters with the* PARROT.)

DERAMO: *(As* OLD MAN*)* Here's Truffaldino's parrot.

ANGELA: I'm certain there's something peculiar about it. And it mentioned magic when it spoke before.

DERAMO: *(As* OLD MAN*)* I still don't understand how this parrot can help us, but I will trust you, my love.

ANGELA: Yes, my dearest, don't fear, we will return you to your original state. If I only I could find out what is so special about this parrot!

(*The* PARROT *remains coy. It's not the right moment, after all.*)

(TARTAGLIA'*s voice is heard.*)

TARTAGLIA: *(As* DERAMO. *Offstage)* Angela! My, my, my sweet! My dearest!

DERAMO: *(As* OLD MAN*)* The voice of the traitor! Oh, my strength, where have you gone?

ANGELA: Go, hide! He'll be here any minute!

(ANGELA *helps* DERAMO-*as*-OLD MAN *to conceal himself offstage; the* PARROT *remains onstage.)*

(TARTAGLIA *enters with* GUARDS; *the* GUARDS *take up positions in the voms.)*

TARTAGLIA: *(As* DERAMO. *To the audience)* I have the stag, I recognize it from its mark; yet I am still full of fear and suspicion. But why? I am the king, everyone trembles!

(ANGELA *reenters.)*

ANGELA: *(To the audience)* How I hate the sight of this traitor! But I must stay calm and try to outsmart him.

TARTAGLIA: *(As* DERAMO. *Catching sight of her)* Angela, Angelina, Angeletta, my heart, my dear, my dove, have those hysterical effects that deprived me of your affection gone? Has your little fit passed?

ANGELA: My lord, I prayed that the heavens would take away the illusion that rendered me so unhappy, and already the cruel abhorrence that I felt has partly vanished from my heart and mind.

TARTAGLIA: *(As* DERAMO. *Taking her by the hand)* My dearest! Brava! Brava! Bravissima! This pleases me—go on.

ANGELA: But then I heard that upon your orders my dear father and sister, poor silly Truffaldino, Brighella, and so many others were barbarously thrown in a harsh prison and my heart failed again. These tyrannical ways were not the ways of Deramo, I said to myself. And once again, I wept. *(She pretends to cry.)*

TARTAGLIA: *(As* DERAMO*)* Do not weep, my dearest. I only placed them in prison to satisfy the people, who are angered by the disappearance of Tartaglia. But, but, but I assure you, I will save your father and sister— after a few interrogations.

ANGELA: *(Aside)* Oh, you traitor!

TARTAGLIA: *(As* DERAMO*)* But, but, but, if by chance their liberation will reawaken your heart more quickly, they shall be free at once. *(To a* GUARD, *grandly)* You there! Leander and Pantalone are to be freed!

*(*TARTAGLIA *silently indicates "not really" to the* GUARD; *the* GUARD *nods and leaves.)*

ANGELA: Dear Deramo, no deed could be more beautiful than this. Already I begin to love you again.

TARTAGLIA: *(As* DERAMO. *In great transports)* Yes! Yes! Yes! Let us go, my Angela.

*(*TARTAGLIA *takes* ANGELA *by the arm; she pulls away.)*

ANGELA: Wait, my dear Deramo, wait—there is only one last teeny, tiny thing that bothers me.

TARTAGLIA: *(As* DERAMO*)* My dove, torment me no longer. Come, come, come, ask me, ask me anything… and let us go.

ANGELA: *(Under her breath, to* TARTAGLIA*)* First, tell these soldiers to go away, my lord.

TARTAGLIA: *(As* DERAMO. *To the remaining* GUARDS*)* Go! Go! Go! Come on, shoo, shoo, shoo!

*(The remaining* GUARDS *leave.)*

ANGELA: My dearest Deramo, to demonstrate your true love and faith, you confided to me this morning your second magic secret—a spell that allowed your spirit to travel into another body. Surely, showing me this magic would be the greatest proof of your love.

TARTAGLIA: *(As* DERAMO. *Aside, surprised)* Curses! Deramo confided his secret to his wife! *(To* ANGELA*)* I would be happy to satisfy you, my heart, but isn't it time for you, after so, so, so many demonstrations of my affection, to repay me in some way?

ANGELA: Dearest Deramo, I assure you, that after this final favor, you will see how capable of love I am. Oh, I know! Why don't you have your guards bring us that stag from the forest?

TARTAGLIA: *(As* DERAMO. *Aside)* This is too much. My suspicions grow without measure. *(To* ANGELA*)* First, give me proof of your love.

ANGELA: Indulge me first, and I am yours.

TARTAGLIA: *(As* DERAMO*)* Oh, I tire of this, you are too ungrateful.

*(*TARTAGLIA *makes various attempts to seize* ANGELA; *she fends him off, until at last they are in a standoff facing each other across the stage.)*

*(*DERAMO-*as*-OLD MAN *enters.)*

DERAMO: *(As* OLD MAN*)* Stop, treacherous villain, stop!

TARTAGLIA: *(As* DERAMO. *Aside)* That sounded like the voice of the king! *(To* ANGELA*)* Oh, traitor! Have you hidden assassins here to take my life?

*(*TARTAGLIA *draws his sword.* ANGELA *places herself in front of* DERAMO-*as*-OLD MAN. TARTAGLIA *regards him in confusion.)*

TARTAGLIA: *(Aside)* Isn't this the old man from the forest? But how can that be? *(To* DERAMO-*as*-OLD MAN*)* Old man, tell me who you are! Tell me, or I will drive this sword into your throat.

DERAMO: *(As* OLD MAN*)* Fiend, look upon me. I am Deramo, your king. The heavens will see that you repent your wickedness.

TARTAGLIA: *(As* DERAMO*)* Guards! Guards! Die, you old liar, and the abyss take you!

*(*GUARDS *armed with quarterstaffs enter and seize* DERAMO-*as*-OLD MAN; TARTAGLIA, *sword drawn,*

*advances on him, but suddenly* LEANDER *and* PANTALONE
*burst onto the scene—they also have quarterstaffs.)*

*(The* GUARDS *let go of* DERAMO *and go for* LEANDER
*and* PANTALONE. PANTALONE *takes on two* GUARDS *at
once, revealing the warrior he once was. An exciting staff
battle occurs.* LEANDER *and* PANTALONE *drive the guards
off. Throughout all this,* TARTAGLIA *is trying to get to
DERAMO-as-*OLD MAN, *but* ANGELA *prevents him. The
PARROT squawks occasional warnings to our heroes.)*

*(*TARTAGLIA *raises his weapon to slay* DERAMO. ANGELA
*struggles with him. There is a sound of a great thunderclap.*
TARTAGLIA, DERAMO, *and* ANGELA *freeze.)*

PARROT: Now, Angela! Release me! Release me!

*(*ANGELA *throws* TARTAGLIA-as-DERAMO *aside and
casts the* PARROT *into the air. Costume magic and special
effects occur. The* PARROT *has vanished. In the* PARROT's
*place stands* DURANDARTE, *holding a magic staff. General
astonishment.)*[17]

DERAMO: *(As* OLD MAN*)* Durandarte!

ANGELA: The magician!

TARTAGLIA: *(As* DERAMO*)* What should I do? Flee?
Attack? Play dead? I cannot think, I am confused and I
tremble!

17      *How we did it: the* DURANDARTE *transformation
resembled the spinning* TARTAGLIA/DERAMO *transformation,
with* CIGOLOTTI *stepping in to assist. In this dreamscape
choreography,* DURANDARTE *spun slowly, handing off his
PARROT puppeteer trappings to* CIGOLOTTI *as* CIGOLOTTI
*removed his own cape and reversed it, placing it on the shoulders
of* DURANDARTE *(the* DURANDARTE *side of the cape was
magnificently and brightly colored). As* DURANDARTE *completed
his final turn,* CIGOLOTTI *threw him his magic staff, which
DURANDARTE caught, completing the transformation.*

(TARTAGLIA *starts to raise his sword;* DURANDARTE *gestures with his staff and* TARTAGLIA *freezes.* DURANDARTE *steps forward.*)

DURANDARTE: Deramo, my friend, be not afraid. Traitorous Tartaglia, tremble and despair! Courageous and clever Angela, rejoice!

TARTAGLIA: *(As* DERAMO*)* Why can't I move? How can I avenge myself! Help! Help! Ministers, servants, soldiers, your king is betrayed!

DURANDARTE: No one can hear you, treacherous minister! Learn now that it is not our outer form that distinguishes us, but our minds and hearts. Yours are so poisonous that no stolen shape can hide your villainy. Deramo's goodness cannot be eclipsed by any change of form. Yet—let the bodies change! *(To* TARTAGLIA*)* Your destiny is upon you, unworthy soul. *(To the others)* Angela, Deramo, and the kingdom, rejoice!

TARTAGLIA: *(As* DERAMO*)* Where can I hide? Where can I run to? Oh, cursed love, cursed ambition, cursed moment that I became a traitor! To the forest! *(He attempts to flee.)*

DURANDARTE: Silence, wicked one! *(He strikes the ground with his staff.)*

(TARTAGLIA-*as*-DERAMO *is turned, with various shrieks and protests, into a* PARROT.)[18]

(DURANDARTE *strikes the ground with his staff.)*

(*The* OLD MAN *casts back his hood and stands tall, revealing that he is* DERAMO *once more.)*

ANGELA: Deramo! My Deramo!

DERAMO: My Angela!

18      *Again, this is achieved through choreographic fabulousness. When the whole business is done, the actor playing* TARTAGLIA *has taken over the puppetry of the* PARROT.

(ANGELA *and* DERAMO *embrace.* DERAMO *turns to* DURANDARTE.)

DERAMO: My friend…how can we thank you enough?

TARTAGLIA: (*As* PARROT) Oh, what misery!

DURANDARTE: Let your fate become a lesson to all, Tartaglia! Open the doors! Summon the people!

(*Strikes the ground with his staff.*)

(*Fabulous final scenic transition here, led by our friend* CIGLIOTTI. *The* GUARDS *assemble to play a triumphant fanfare.*)

(*Everyone rushes on.*)

TARTAGLIA: (*As* PARROT) Friends, I am Tartaglia! Tartaglia! Tartaglia! Transformed into this feathered creature. I have been a wicked, wicked man. Pity me!

(*General astonishment*)

CLARISSA: Oh, my father…my poor father…

TARTAGLIA: (*As* PARROT) Do not cry, daughter; I am not worthy of tears.

(CLARISSA *gently gathers the* PARROT *to her protectively.*)

Daughter. Clarissa.

PANTALONE: I don't know which is stronger right now—fear, joy, or the curiosity to understand these mysteries!

LEANDER: I have become a stone. I understand nothing.

ANGELA: Father, sister, friends, I understand your amazement. But we must wait for a better time to tell you all.

DERAMO: Illustrious magician, you have saved us—my kingdom is yours if you will have it.

DURANDARTE: Durandarte has no interest in kingdoms. I will return to the forest—where no beast seeks dominion over its fellow creatures. This land belongs to you, and to your people, and it is the people who together must keep their land safe from tyranny. And now, as we promised at the beginning of this evening, it is time to raise a toast!

*(Various groupings assemble.)*

*(*DERAMO *and* ANGELA—*a reunification.)*

*(*CLARISSA, LEANDER, *and a beaming* PANTALONE—*the* PARROT *is still with them—a family.)*

*(*SMERALDINA *and* TRUFFALDINO's *eyes meet. They sidle toward each other—a reconciliation.)*

*(*BRIGHELLA *and* CIGLIOTTI's *eyes meet. They also sidle toward each other—a beginning.)*

DURANDARTE: *(To the audience)* Let evil everywhere be vanquished! Let love flourish! May everyone find their hearts' desires and may there be health, happiness, and, especially, peace—for all humankind! All we need now is an ending to our story, and that, if you will be so kind, will now be provided by you!

*(Music. Rain of white petals)*

### END OF PLAY